How To Intern Successfully

Insights and Actions
to Optimize your Experience

Robert J. Khoury

with *John Selby*

Printed in the United States of America

ISBN-13: 978-1-956503-00-5 print edition
ISBN-13: 978-1-956503-01-2 ebook edition

Waterside Productions
2055 Oxford Ave, Cardiff, CA 92007
www.waterside.com

Acknowledgements

~~~~~~~~~~~~~~~~~~~~~~~~~~~~~~

This book is hopefully the first of many to come. And, happily, I didn't do it alone. I first of all want to thank everyone who has interned with me over the years, starting with Sharad Kumar in 2004. Each taught me life lessons I treasure. I especially acknowledge Mohammed Eazad for inspiring me to create an internship program second to none, and also Emilie Szemraj.

I thank my cousin Nabil Freij for setting up my first internship in 1988. His kindness is heartfelt and genuine. And I thank my children, William and Eloise, for their love, support and verve for life. I thank my wife Mary for saying "Yes". Because of her, I know miracles happen. If there is reincarnation, I will come back and marry her again.

I thank my parents, Salwa and Nabil, for providing me with everything I have ever needed in life. Their generous, loving spirit, coupled with their strong moral character, make them extraordinary role models for all who know them.

Finally I acknowledge my friend and mentor John Selby for collaborating with me from start to finish and making this book possible. His ability to bring grace and ease to this challenging endeavor made all the difference. Without John this work would not exist. Thank you.

~~~~~~~~~~~~~~~~~~~~~~~~~~~~

If you believe passionately
in what you are doing
and whom you are doing it with,
then success is bound to follow.

Anisa Kamadoli Costa

Table Of Contents

~~~~~~~~~~~~~~~~~~~~~~~

We are what we repeatedly do.
Excellence is not an act,
it's a habit.

Aristotle

Prologue
Why Interning Is For You

~~~~~~~~~~~~~~~~~~~~~~~

Value your time and
do what is valuable.

Dalai Lama

Over a million college students in America do an internship every year. In addition, almost two million students advance into graduate programs and essentially intern within that context. And for every intern, there's a corporate or academic mentor who takes on the responsibility of making the intern's experience both satisfying and rewarding for all parties involved.

As a successful businessman who regularly brings college students into my company for summer, winter-break, and semester internships, I aim with this book to share what I've learned about how to have a meaningful (and also quite enjoyable) intern experience within the world of business. I'll be speaking mostly to the corporate intern experience, but the discussions readily translate into grad student situations.

The whole process of diving into deep engagement with a company or graduate program can be a somewhat scary experience. This discussion will make sure you fully understand each step of the intern process, and successfully move through these steps into an experience of personal growth, rapid learning, and stimulating discoveries. As you engage with supportive mentors who've been advancing their own careers for decades and now want to pass it on, you'll gain essential insights and priceless experiences.

I also intend for this text to encourage and inform managers and mentors, by putting them into an intern's shoes so that they better understand what an intern wants and needs. Being a mentor to an intern is a deep responsibility, as I've found out for myself. This book will hopefully make a difference for both interns and their mentors as they learn to work harmoniously together.

The goal of an internship is for both parties to share perspectives and benefit equally from the relationship – so that the intern flourishes and so does the hosting company or institution. As one recent intern named Caroline put it:

"My intern/mentor relationship was one of the most important experiences in my college-student life. These early business experiences have the power to impact an intern quite deeply. More specifically, a purposefully-designed and compassionately-administered internship program like Rob provides can reveal new realms of business life. A good mentor can ensure that the intern feels confident to take the risks necessary to grow and succeed."

The intern experience from start to finish can be either an anxious stressful unsatisfying bore – or a most wonderfully stimulating and rewarding opportunity. I personally went through college and into the business world with very limited support during my internships – so I want to share with you some of the insights and guidance I wish I myself had received. Life is all about both giving and receiving. As an experienced intern mentor I'm pleased to offer whatever I have to share. I'm here to help you optimize your intern adventure.

Each of us must work for our own improvement,
and at the same time share
a general responsibility
for all humanity.

Marie Curie

Examining Your Motivations

These days, if you're interested in a corporate career, interning is usually how you're expected to spend your college summers. It seems that for many college students, the initial motivation to do an internship emerges from the assumptions that interning is just one of those many college things you're supposed to do. Probably some of your classmates are seeking internships. Meanwhile, older students are perhaps talking about what a great (or not so great) experience they recently had through interning. Naturally you don't want to feel left behind, you want your summer breaks to be productive – so you're determined to make the necessary effort to land a worthwhile intern position.

You'll find a variety of internships being offered, from shorter winter-break and summer internships to lengthier semester and full-year internships. Upwards of a million college students in the U.S. will intern this year. And often, a student's internship is a trial that might lead to future employment. About half of all internships are unpaid. If you can get a summer internship at one of the top Silicon Valley companies or perhaps a financial firm in New York, you'll definitely be ahead of the crowd. But the reality is that there's so much competition for those positions, you'll probably need to set realistic expectations while also aiming for the top.

Compensation-wise, a few tech companies like Google and Facebook pay interns up to ten grand a month, but the average intern wage is around fifteen bucks an hour. That's obviously not going to be a financial windfall – so your main motivators should be the experience itself and the hope of future career advancement. A good internship will enhance your resume. You'll look good for having gone out and gained experience in a career that you aspire toward.

All of this is in stark contrast to the past when summer was meant for relaxation, rejuvenation, family time, enjoying your vacation – and maybe even some romance if it came your way. That old scenario is long gone for most students. Usually the pressures to get ahead are too high to allow you to 'waste' a summer – and besides, interning can be fun. Interning offers you a novel chance to break beyond mundane student routines and discover remarkable new dimensions of yourself and business life, as well as things you won't learn in the classroom.

Another major reason to intern is to learn more about the dynamics of teamwork – how to engage in the process of dedicated group action. Interning can help you transcend the isolated ego boundaries of student identity. You've perhaps noticed how being at college can be a seriously solo experience. You alone must prepare for and take your tests. Compare that to the business reality where success is often determined by your ability to be a harmonious contributor to a cooperative team. During an internship you'll learn how to work under a boss and fit into a corporate culture. It's also a chance to experiment with 'managing upward' and influencing the people around you in work situations. You'll learn that there's always someone above you who is in command. And you'll experiment both with being a follower and a leader on a team.

Business is all about a different mode of communication than you've been immersed in during your school years. In an internship you'll be able to observe yourself as an adult responding to many new suggestions, instructions, guidance, criticism and all the rest. You'll see how your current communication habits work for you, and discover where they don't, as you adapt to meet each new situation.

Of equal importance, while interning you can discover whether you're truly attracted to a career in a particular sector of an industry. Some professions may seem highly desirable, like investment banking or entrepreneurship or consulting – but they might not map onto you personally once you actually get inside and explore them. The only way to know what suits your driving passion in business is to get out there and experience it first-hand.

> *Perhaps right now you might want to pause for a few moments and reflect a bit on why you yourself are thinking of interning. What are your motivations, your concerns, your hopes and expectations?*

Discovering Who You Really Are

Establishing your deeper identity and life purpose is a long-term process that will continue throughout your life. You might know who you are when at home with your friends, or in school, or on vacation – but who will you be in the world of business? Never before have students faced a more complex, confusing and often upsetting world. The future on all fronts is unpredictable, with challenging new developments regularly overwhelming youthful hopes and dreams.

As you know, college life doesn't automatically come with experienced mentors and helpful life training to support your inner struggle for self-growth and actualization. College life is too often presented in movies and in the media as nonstop fun and partying – but in reality you probably got to college and felt quite alone in a seemingly-vast crowd of mostly self-absorbed fellow students. And although you might try to stay tough emotionally and project a cool façade, deep-down your college life can be really challenging, to say the least.

Interning can provide an opportunity to wake up to your true emerging self. A recent intern named Anlin put it this way: "I think that we should go into an internship with an open mind and embrace the different opportunities that arise along the way. Be ready to continually learn and grow – and most importantly, just be yourself rather than someone you think your business host is looking for. I learned first-hand as an intern that it's always best to present yourself genuinely."

As we'll see in this book, even before going off for your internship you can make definite steps into adulthood and career advancement. Your college years are all about beginning to discover who you actually are and what gives you true satisfaction. And this self-discovery is something you'll want to be actively pursuing, in order to wake up to your higher professional and career potential.

Most corporations will expect you to have grown up before entering the workforce. They don't want to manage you like they do their children. They want to hire an adult. Therefore it's essential to spend time on your own inner development – both before doing an internship, and also while moving through an intern experience. "Know yourself" isn't an outdated cliché – it's a continual call to action. In this spirit, an intern adventure can be your chance to mature at an accelerated pace by encountering new challenging experiences that push you beyond your familiar comfort zones.

That said, it's usually a mistake to act totally grown up when you're still in the process of getting there. Good mentors know that most college student interns are still emerging from their cocoon. What's important is being honest – and open to learning, growing, and letting go as you advance gracefully through your internal maturation process.

In actual practice, you'll find that you can't separate the world beyond you from the world inside you – your experience of life is always a melding of the two. Often you can't change your external situation – but you can definitely learn to change your inner feelings, your ingrained attitudes, and your worldview. As you advance your inner perspective, you'll find that your outer world changes in tandem. Both before and during an internship you can explore all of this in action.

Maturity is about realizing that there are definite choices you can make in life about what you want your world to look like and what goals you want to evolve toward. You'll find that those choices have real consequences in your future. Going from high school to college is certainly a major leap, but that leap remains mostly confined within your student routines and family expectations. You're still preparing yourself for entering the real world.

When you do an internship, you'll become free to explore beyond the bounds of the student mindset – you gain the opportunity to grow beyond the confines of your past life. No longer enmeshed in the culture of a college campus where you're studying day and night, you can witness yourself intimately engaged with a world where important events are unfolding. And you'll experience for yourself that your work can make a difference in the real world.

As a leader with the Princeton Club of Chicago, a decade ago I started organizing summer intern luncheons for interested

Princeton students in the Chicago area. Then I took the leap and started hiring interns of my own. As I set aside time and energy to welcome students into my company, a whole new world opened up for me. I had no idea what I'd get out of being a mentor to students within the business environment – and I also had no idea specifically what I would contribute.

Mentoring interns proved to be a most enlightening expansion of my own world. I had limited intern experiences in college, so I wasn't confident about where I was headed after I graduated. Only when I entered the business world as an experience, not just an idea or an image, did I start to realize how much I didn't know I didn't know.

Luckily during my first years in business, I was guided by lots of people who were ahead of me in life – managers who were patient with me, who saw my potential and eagerness to learn. If you can engage with such mentors while still in college through selecting an internship that suits your particular needs, you'll be positioned well for success in business and life.

> *It's what you learn*
> *after you know it all*
> *that counts.*

John Wooden

Preparing For Your Sherpa To Find You

Perhaps a good metaphor for the intern experience is that of climbing a challenging mountain without having personally had the experience of climbing such a mountain. In this type of situation, if possible, it's always wise to have a Sherpa as a hands-on guide – someone who's been there and is willing (and eager) to assist you in your adventure of manifesting your goals. Through developing a bond of trust, compassion, teamwork and pleasure in the climb, intern and mentor can work together and succeed in the challenge.

I very much love working in person with interns. I also want to be supportive to as many students as possible – thus this book format that can reach many at once. I very much want to see more people getting to the mountain top. And I want to encourage a process where everyone can come to know themselves as winners. A well-thought-out internship design can augment this process.

The business world is evolving rapidly, I have high hopes for our shared future. Each of us can quite actively influence corporate evolution as we strive to create a clearer, more authentic and inclusive approach to making a living – a genuine win-win game in the workplace. In this spirit, I want interns to be more highly valued as fresh spirits offering new ideas and perspectives. We need to see the intern presence as an opportunity to expand the whole notion of what business is all about. After all, they are learning the latest technologies and innovative ideas in their colleges. Given half a chance, interns can bring in vital new ways of looking at the world of commerce.

Unfortunately, anticipating an internship can also be scary, a process that must be somehow endured, beginning with a series of upsetting interviews leading you toward a bothersome stepping stone into a boring career. But I assure you, interning can also be your big chance to break free and grow. It can be an exciting adventure that launches a lifetime of fulfilling work. You've got to start wherever you are – and trust your own instincts and intentions to help you tap into the deeper learning experience of the intern situation as you move through it.

Reading this book will provide a first taste of what an intern experience might offer you. Will your real-life experience in a challenging at-work situation awaken your inner power and untapped potential? Right now, when you look inward, what emotions are being evoked by the very idea of leaving campus and going off into an intern assignment? Would you say you are feeling confident and eager to do an internship? Or are you perhaps feeling anxious, worried and possibly inadequate for the task?

Without judging what you find, just observe your current emotions. Be entirely honest with yourself – and see if you can begin to let go of unwanted attitudes and reactions about interning. Begin the process we'll be exploring later in this book of actively choosing which feelings, attitudes and goals you consciously want to welcome into your life.

Here's a final preliminary thought. Wise employers and managers hire interns in order to interact with and better understand the new generation. Our culture is changing dramatically, seemingly overnight, and college interns can bring the unique insights and perspectives of their upsurging generation right into the workplace. Successful companies know they need to have their finger on the pulse of what's coming – and interns can alert corporations to future challenges, attitudes and trends.

Today's college students represent a tech-driven, ecologically-concerned, socially-conscious culture that's never before been seen on this planet – and through purposefully hosting interns, companies have the opportunity to tap early into what's going on in young minds and hearts. What do they value, how do they perceive their emerging world?

During the roughly twenty years since today's college students were born, there's been so much drastic change throughout our global community. How has all of this impacted this new generation which is set to take over the reins of power and commerce in the next decades? A company can hire an intern or two and perhaps find out!

For our own success to be real
it must contribute to the
success of others.

Eleanor Roosevelt

Chapter One

PREPARING FOR THE ADVENTURE

~~~~~~~~~~~~~~~~~~~~~~~

Tell me and I forget.
Teach me and I may remember.
Involve me and I will learn.

Confucius

Beginning with your first communication with a company about an internship, the underlying dynamic is clear – you're initiating a dance between you and the people on the other side. And when you find a successful work situation where both sides of this equation are equal and harmonious, when feelings are mutually receptive and out in the open, then you've probably discovered a good fit.

This relationship is what I've been exploring from my 'company side' of the equation – particularly how best to bring these two opposite roles of student intern and company mentor into congruence. An intern named Mohammed expressed the congruence this way:

"I very much value authenticity and experience in a mentor – someone who is much more experienced than myself on many fronts. However, experience alone doesn't make a great mentor. Openness and sharing are also crucial qualities for both mentor and intern. Being authentic and constantly promoting transparency with one another is something I greatly value in the intern/mentor relationship."

Ideally this dynamic manifests right at the beginning of the company/student encounter. If both of you are being authentic and upfront, kind to each other and receptive, then the internship is free to flow naturally into a good experience for both parties. But keep in mind that your prevailing expectations and assumptions at the beginning will mostly determine the outcome. This is why I'm encouraging you to take a look at your existing mindset about interning first, so that this element can evolve before you begin interviewing.

I graduated high school at the top of my class academically and a captain of two sports. Everything in my life was flowing as if by magic. Naively, it seemed that I could do no wrong. But I now realize that my expectations when heading off to college were completely unrealistic – that is, quite ungrounded in reality. I graduated from a small private school with 42 other male classmates and then went off to a top-tier university with over a thousand students per class – and yet I expected to have the same kind of experience I'd had in high school. I assumed I'd be seen as a hot shot and that I would readily succeed in anything I took on at Princeton.

My unrealistic expectations led to a bunch of frustrating failures. I tried to jump into half a dozen different activities on campus along with my studies – and I mostly fell flat on my face. It was a humbling experience, to say the least. And I think many of my classmates had similar feelings. I guess that's just part of the college process as students encounter tough competition and humbly have to begin to look for their unique paths to success – finding their niche rather than pretending they're a master of all trades.

Later on, many years after college, I heard someone speak at a conference, a football player from another top-tier university. He said that when he went off to college his dad said to him: "You have the opportunity to be excellent in academics, you can have an extraordinary athletic experience, and you can have a ton of fun with an incredible social life. But you're going to have to pick just two of those and no more, if you want to seriously succeed in college."

Unwisely, I did the opposite and the stress was too much, the competition was too high, and there just wasn't enough time or energy for more than two full-time engagements on campus. I learned my lesson the hard way. I was suddenly on the world stage, no longer in some prep school bubble. The academic challenge in college itself was gigantic and being on the wrestling team was equally so. The commitment involved was incredible in terms of time, stamina, dedication and so forth. But I also wanted to excel socially and make lots of lifelong like-minded friends. That led me to join and become an officer in Cap and Gown, a social and eating club. I also got involved in extracurriculars like the debating society.

And … it was too much. By the time I graduated, had I actually succeeded academically, athletically, socially and extra-curricularly? The answer was absolutely no. In all four directions, my self-confidence had in fact progressively collapsed – and it took me at least half a dozen years to get my confidence back. Of course, a few students can take on more than two major commitments at a time in college, but for most people, it's wise not to overextend. You might think that stuffing your resume with college activities is a plus – but in my experience, most companies are not looking for a flashy jack of all trades. Companies are looking for someone who can commit to one challenge and get the job done superlatively for the duration.

Life itself isn't only about collecting a bunch of academic awards and intellectual accomplishments. It's also all about enjoying the journey – all the discoveries and feelings and opportunities that arise along the way. Growing up has a lot of traumas that impinge on our development. College is hopefully a time when we begin to become self-observant, when we catch our unrealistic or even neurotic reactions to situations, and learn ways to transcend them.

One of my personal challenges in college was that I was a year younger than most of my classmates. In fact, I would have been young for the class one year after mine. My parents decided to put me ahead a year after a sudden return to the U.S. because of the outbreak of the Lebanese civil war in 1975. This event led to unresolved fears that surfaced in college.

My parents are immigrants to the U.S. and in 1973 they decided to settle back in southwest Asia in Beirut. I was four years old and I loved our new home, especially living in the same building as aunts, uncles and cousins. The outbreak of the civil war changed everything. Now danger and violence entered my early childhood and I naturally picked up a lot of frightful feelings. We left Beirut abruptly for Jordan where we stayed with relatives until my parents could arrange our return to the U.S.

While we were living in Jordan and I was in kindergarten, my aunt commented that I was pretty bright and should skip a grade when we move back to the States. So – I never did first grade. I remember showing up at school in second grade at St. Mary's Academy Bay View in East Providence, RI and not knowing what was going on at all. I struggled hard to catch up. And even in college, I was still carrying worries that I was behind others in many of life's lessons. I also still had lingering fearful emotions after living in a war zone.

In my observation, most of us during childhood experienced some sort of trauma or struggle that we then had to try to overcome as we grew up. Our early years were full of seen and unseen obstacles and shocks that dented or damaged our personalities. Our prevailing attitudes and expectations became tainted with emotional inhibitions and mental distortions that put limits on our outlook. We often overcompensated for something or developed anxieties that we sometimes carried all the way into college.

When we survive and transcend such struggles, we can grow stronger. But we need to regularly reflect on whether we're still carrying defensive apprehensions that hold us back. It's definitely a good idea to deal with such challenging and self-defeating feelings before going off for an internship.

> *You might want to reflect a bit on this: what difficulties and struggles did you have while you were growing up? And do they continue to bother you in your college days?*

If you want, you can put this book aside for a few minutes, relax and reflect – and see what comes to mind in this regard. What attitudes or undesirable emotions might you still be carrying that could limit your internship experience? And what might you do, in order to actively let go of past traumas so that you can truly shine in your internship?

Pause & Reflect

~~~~~~~~~~~~~~~~~~~~~~~

Striving Toward Autonomy

Most of us yearn to be free in life, to be in charge of our own destiny. Taking part in an internship can be the first step as you move in the direction of autonomy. It usually takes a person quite a long time to achieve autonomy – but you can accelerate this process by consciously endeavoring to be more self-directed.

Being autonomous doesn't mean that you don't have to answer to someone. Everyone answers to someone. Really. You might be the richest person on the planet but when you go home from your office, you might have to answer to your wife or your partner or your best friend. And at the office you might have to answer to the chairman of the board. Everyone answers to somebody because we live within society, and that means we're all interdependent. But the relative feeling of autonomy is something that can uplift the spirit to a new level of freedom you aspire toward.

It's taken me decades to achieve a deep sense of autonomy. Like everyone else, in early childhood I was totally dependent on my parents for my comfort and survival. We all begin without any autonomy at all, that's the biological reality of life – and then over time, if all goes well, we move toward greater and greater freedom. We learn how to make our own decisions and earn our own keep and take care of ourselves.

At Princeton my parents were still paying my bills. And they had expectations attached to supporting me in college. I didn't feel free for instance to choose my own major and direction in life. When I went home midway through freshman year I was all excited about art history. Along with my math and science courses that were required for an electrical engineering degree, I'd taken an art history class and I'd absolutely loved it. But for my parents, majoring in art history was a nonstarter. And while they were paying my education bills, I had to answer to them.

Most of us go through a period in college where we're still dependent on someone to cover our expenses for four years – and we're thankful for that support – but we also begin to want the freedom to decide what we're going to do when we wake up in the morning. We can taste a bit of freedom – but we know where our boundaries lie.

Then, if we manage to get into an internship, we come face to face with another authority figure, our manager or mentor in the company where we're interning for the summer, winter, or semester. We gain some freedom in that we're out of the school situation. We're free to have new experiences and strengthen our ability to do work and support ourselves. We gain new responsibilities in life and it feels good to be out in the real world and not locked up in old school habits.

In school, whether you realize it or not, you are locked into a linear flow of development that you have no control over. You started in kindergarten and went right through grade twelve. Then college continued that same linear progression. Then you're in an internship and you feel free of all the restrictions of being in school. You're more on your own. That can feel good, and it can also feel unsettling or disorienting. Like I said, gaining autonomy takes time. When you're an intern you gain some freedoms – and you learn that with the freedom comes new responsibility.

Especially if you have a good mentor in your work situation, you will be given a lot of new freedom to make decisions on your own and to take some responsibility for what you do with a client. A good manager will make sure an intern feels involved in decisions and gains a sense of being able to influence the flow of the company's evolution. One of my interns offered this comment:

"Rob made sure that we interns were transitioning quickly from a school mindset into his company's start-up mindset. We were encouraged to think outside the box and come up with new ideas to grow the company. The overall intern experience felt like an adventure as we learned from one another, grew together, and finished the summer as more confident individuals."

In my opinion, along with offering a sense of stability and security in the workplace, a good manager needs to also provide interns with a sense of opportunity, choice and adventure. Gaining expanded freedom always involves gaining uncertainty: you're free to make decisions and that involves taking on risk. Being autonomous means you're in charge of your life. That can be challenging and uncomfortable, but ultimately rewarding.

Life shrinks or expands
in proportion to one's courage.

Anais Nin

Creating Your Own Future

One thing you'll almost certainly encounter when you start an internship is uncertainty – in a company, anything can happen. In the face of uncertainty, the wise move is to learn how to begin to anticipate change. You begin to evaluate your situation and make very short-term predictions about what might happen. Based on those predictions, you can decide which outcome you want to work toward manifesting.

That's how you create your own future – you take responsibility for where you're at and you look to see which direction you want to move. What inspires you? What attracts you? What seems most possible and desirable? Rather than just listening to what your parents and teachers are advising you to do, you start listening to your own inner voice – and you begin to trust that inner voice and act on it.

While in college you can consciously learn to nurture an ever-expanding vision of where you yourself want to go in your future. You also begin to take specific actions that are consistent with your vision, whatever it might be. You can learn to decide what's most important in your life, and regularly evaluate what comes first.

For my own life, I have step by step developed a business where I feel in charge and adequately autonomous. I love my clients, they're great, but they don't determine what I choose to do. Clients can fire me, that's fine, and equally importantly I can fire them. Why does that matter? Because when push comes to shove, it's my family that determines my decisions. For me, family comes first, period. I don't allow travel demands to interfere with my being available and tuned into my kids. I know what comes first. And I feel that even in college you can begin to develop what your own priorities are and commit yourself to honoring those priorities.

Many times in your future you're going to have to make what seem to be limiting decisions. Are you going to be someone who is at home with the family, or are you going to put career over family and be gone most of the time? Are you always going to take the highest salary being offered, or are you going to consider other factors when advancing your career? Even during your internship you'll encounter various people and situations pulling you in divergent directions. You'll have to start inquiring for yourself about upcoming decisions based on your interior set of values and goals.

A well-designed internship will provide you with numerous opportunities to make decisions that you're responsible for. This is very valuable life practice. Ultimately no one else can make key life choices for you – unless you yield that power.

And that's not a wise idea if you're interested in autonomy. Early on, you'll want to purposefully develop a firm foundation of personal integrity and responsibility. You might end up with a great mentor in your internship who gives you maximum autonomy in your assignments – or you might have to temporarily submit to a manager who dominates. In either case you're going to learn a great deal that will help illuminate your decisions later on.

> *However good or bad a situation is*
> *... it will change.*

> **Regina Brett**

What You Can't Control

There are two things that you usually can't determine for yourself in your early adult work life. One is your calendar, your schedule. Someone else is usually controlling that – your manager, your boss, your family obligations and so on. As an employee you must submit to what other people want you to do when they want it done. You must be where they want you to be when they want you to be there. It takes time and intent to advance in life to where you feel free to set your own calendar.

But you can step by step strive toward autonomy. In my current business life in my fifties, there's nothing at all on my calendar that I didn't happily put there. I've reached one of my goals in life – it took time and it wasn't easy. I had to be intentional in order to achieve this goal. But it was worth it in order to feel that I'm fully in charge of my life. I do what feels good and right and satisfying with my time.

You can choose to aim your future in that direction, if it speaks to you. Even right now, you're already in charge of your personal long-term intentions. What's important is realizing that you have this freedom. You can assume full responsibility for aiming your life where you truly want to go. Right now and forever after, each choice you make with conscious intent will be important! So know what you are aiming for in your career as you make choices each day.

The second thing that you'll probably have little control over in your twenties will be who you interact with. For instance you'll be assigned a manager or mentor during your internship. You can choose what company you're going to intern with, but then you must follow whomever you get as a manager in that company. And you'll be given assignments and clients to work with. This is simply a given aspect of the process of advancing upward in a company.

Some people will drag you down, others will pick you up – you'll encounter all kinds in the workplace. If you accept your situation for the time being, you'll definitely learn a great deal along your path toward autonomy. Set your intention to become more and more autonomous as time goes by, this situation won't last forever. I no longer interact with anyone I don't want to. It is definitely possible to advance to where you control both your calendar and the people you're spending your time with, day in and day out. But to do so takes operating in life with a very high level of integrity.

I've found that when I feel free, and the people I'm relating with feel free, we all become more energized and productive and fulfilled in our work. This is a proven fact – when everyone on a team experiences a sense of freedom, responsibility, commitment, satisfaction and happiness, they do better work in less time. The feeling of autonomy at work isn't some vague irrational dream, it's simply the best way to run a successful company. When you enter a company temporarily as an intern, you can evaluate that company based on an autonomy scale you create, and see for yourself the degree of freedom in the workplace.

The love of liberty is the love of others;
the love of power is the love of ourselves.

William Hazlitt

What Do You Really Want?

In a family, usually it's the parents who make most decisions for their young children. Then over time day by day the children begin to assume some responsibility for themselves. In some cultures, children assume responsibility for themselves very early – but in our complex society, this happens later on.

When you yourself finally went off to college, you made a major step into autonomy. When you graduate and get your own job and place, you'll make another leap into self-regulation. An intern experience is a dress-rehearsal for this step. Thrust into a new environment with new rules and responsibilities and unique opportunities for self-expression, you'll discover previously unseen aspects of who you are and what you like.

Again, self-awareness is key through all of this. I hope with this book to encourage you to start asking "Who am I?" regularly, in all sorts of different circumstances. Especially with domineering parents, many children don't realize that they can ask the question, "What do I really want?" Too often, children are expected to just go along with what their parents consider best for them. For example, did you really pick your religion?

You are your own unique case study – and when you're in college, you have the chance finally to take a breather and find out who you are as a distinct unique personality. This is a process that takes self-reflection and time. If you want to know who you are, what you like, what you want in life and what you definitely don't want, you have to observe your own thoughts, your own emotions, your own habits and actions. When your parents aren't present, when you're outside your childhood surroundings, when you're free to be yourself – who are you? Especially, who are you for yourself when no one is around?

I'm not suggesting that you sit around judging yourself. Actually I'm suggesting just the opposite – that you look to see who you really are, without judging yourself at all! Just look and find out the truth of who you naturally are, when you're free to just be you. Hopefully this process will let you begin to accept yourself and love yourself just as you are. Only then can you begin to ask yourself what you really want in life.

Often college students find that they feel stuck – stuck in their parents' attitudes and beliefs, stuck in unspoken assumptions about their limitations, stuck in a life trajectory that isn't really theirs at all but rather belongs to their parents, teachers, friends and relatives. They might feel resigned to parental and societal expectations, or feel rebellious, or get depressed. One way or another, the only way out of these inherited limitations is to take some risks and actually do something – begin exploring new feelings and ideas, expectations and possibilities.

Doing an internship is an optimal way to act, to try something new – and perhaps start to break free. Ideally, before you take off on an internship adventure, you'll have started to ask yourself, over and over again, key questions that will shed light on the path you want to walk in life.

This might be a good time to practice this process so that it becomes second-nature to be self-reflective. If you want, you can pause in reading this book for a few moments or minutes, and explore what comes to mind when you, honestly and without judgment, ask yourself the following questions. Keep in mind that your current answers aren't really as important as learning to consciously turn your attention away from the outside world and direct it inward ... to observe your own feelings, your own thoughts, apprehensions and aspirations:

> *First of all, tune in to your experience of your breathing –*
> *because your inner feelings are always reflected in your*

breathing … and also notice how you feel in your heart. Your feelings are centered in your heart and those feelings deeply influence the thoughts you think …

And after perhaps ten to twelve deep relaxed breaths, just see what comes effortlessly to mind when you say to yourself each of these questions in turn, taking a few breaths for each question:

"Who am I when I'm not doing anything?"

"Why am I in college?"

"What's missing right now in my life?"

"What do I want to be doing in a few years?"

"Who could I be if I stopped worrying?"

"What is most important in my life?"

"Who is most important in my life?"

"Why do I want to do an internship?"

"How might interning change me for the better?"

Pause & Reflect

~~~~~~~~~~~~~~~~~~~~~~~~

Chapter Two

FINDING YOUR WAVE
~~~~~~~~~~~~~~~~~~~

Success comes from surrounding yourself
with people that are at least
as smart as you are.

J.B. Fuqua

I think every college student and every intern is hoping to find abundance in their future. But what is abundance, really – and how in fact do we attain abundance in our lives? To reflect on this question and gain a realistic sense of where abundance is to be found seems an essential aspect of college education. But of course, it's not usually talked about very much at all. Let's take a look at how the intern experience can begin to stimulate the flow of abundance in your life.

The key thing I've learned about abundance is that if you truly want it, you yourself must act – you must create it! If you sit around expecting anyone else to create your abundance, good luck – that won't happen. So, how are you going to create abundance?

Well, clearly to create anything at all, you're going to need the skills required to create it – and those skills might be different than what you thought they were. For instance, you're going to need to develop the skill of listening. If you don't know everything you need to know in order to generate abundance, first you're going to need to take the time to be quiet and listen to people who might know that kind of information. It's that simple. Every day, pay attention to how well you listen to people in general. Begin to seek out and listen to people who might have the answers and insights you need.

There's also the skill of discernment – in particular, the skill of discerning opportunity. If you want to bring abundance into your life, you're going to need the skill of identifying situations where you might have a chance to advance, to discover, to enter into new circles and spheres of influence where abundance is to be found. You need to sharpen your hunting abilities so that you know what you're looking for, and can discern hints of its presence around you. That's why you need to go to work on yourself – so that you can successfully move in the direction where abundance is to be found. You'll find that working on yourself will reduce the number of times that you get in your own way.

We live in a marvelous world where there's always abundance with everything. But we do not relate to the world that way. We bring the view that what is real is scarcity, including in our own careers. What we don't realize is that we tend to get out of life exactly what we expect to get out of it. We get what we ask for, and also quite unfortunately, what we're afraid of. Again, self-inquiry is the skill that can break us out of the bonds of scarcity.

Ultimately, scarcity arises when we're lazy, or when we're bored, or when we're anxious. Each of these mental and emotional states will freeze our ability to look around us, to think beyond what we don't have, and seek out new approaches to our situation. Once we make the effort to look around us in new ways, we discover that there's a lot of abundance and opportunity right in front of us all the time.

But you have to really look hard at what's right in front of you to discover what you seek, what you need, and what you say you deserve in life. There is the old adage, "Seek and you will find; knock and the door will open for you." But you gotta seek, you gotta knock! And like the Rolling Stones said in a song, "You gotta move!" Inaction both physically and mentally is what generates scarcity.

You need to shift your attitudes and related emotions beyond the grip of perceived scarcity if you want to open up to abundance. The false 'scarcity' assumption – that there's not enough goods for everyone to live a good life – generates negative feelings of hopelessness, self-doubt, worry, blame and so forth. The empowering 'abundance' assumption generates feelings of optimism, courage, faith, joy and compassion. If you actively cultivate these positive emotions, you move your whole life trajectory toward abundance. Again, it's not easy – but with time you will find that the rewards are truly extraordinary.

Depending on your mood and prevailing emotions, you see the world either with eyes that see limitations and resignation, or with eyes looking beyond the obvious and assumed, toward new possibilities and openings for action. We tend to walk past opportunities every day but fail to recognize them because we're not looking at the world around us with the right spirit.

If you feel optimistic about abundance existing all around you, you'll begin to discover that abundance – it's that simple in theory, even though it can be a challenge in practice. You will further yourself by putting in the effort to think and feel and explore in a new mode regarding what is and what isn't possible. Break beyond the paradigm of scarcity. See what happens when you regularly say to yourself: "All I see around me is abundance." By reinforcing that perspective you can actively create a future of freedom and joy.

Discovering Your Niche

There is an old saying: "By limiting your scope, you expand your success." Any business you might intern with will be following this rule – they've identified a market niche and they're working to be the best in that niche. They're not trying to do everything at once for everyone. They're striving to be outstanding with a particular great product they're producing at minimum cost. That's the heart of capitalism, and of all entrepreneurial ventures.

Limitations and constraints exist everywhere. Companies that succeed are continually looking for new ways to push beyond those perceived limitations and constraints. When you intern, you'll be expected to play in this game of improving the company's niche product or service to increase revenue, or perhaps assisting in finding new ways to reduce costs. You'll do this through seeking new opportunities with technology, communication, finance, operations, or other important functions. If you train yourself to look for opportunities, you'll find them.

Seen another way, if you maintain the right inner spirit of exploration within your niche, you're going to naturally attract what you're seeking. This means you're going to do two things – you're going to focus outward for new opportunity and you're going to focus inward to keep your inner charge of curiosity, courage and abundance burning hot. You're going to develop your talents and positive stance in your niche and, when the time is right, you're going to be discovered as an asset. Why? Because you are embodying the spirit of abundance that your company seriously needs in order to succeed.

Even before you arrive at a company for your internship, you'll want to study the industry you'll be entering, and your particular company's niche. Explore this niche and see if it resonates with your budding career interests. In this spirit, I do my best as a mentor to let my interns select projects that reflect a niche they're interested in exploring. Lauren, one of my early interns, mentioned in her review of her intern experience that "Rob allowed us the choice to work on and lead projects that we found most empowering." And I find that when I let interns choose their own focus, they do their very best.

By the time you arrive for your intern experience, make sure you're prepared with basic facts and ideas about the industry. What is the big picture? Why does this company even exist? As much as you can, develop whatever particular skills the company might value. And discover where new possibilities are opening for that company. That's a potential path to abundance.

Also, see if you can engage with someone in that company who is already well-grounded in the spirit and operation of abundance. Observe them, learn from them, identify and develop the related skills they've mastered. That's where you want to be – within the aura of a master of abundance, of positive outlook, of courage and trust in a rewarding outcome. You'll find that these bright lights in a company are also willing to share their abundance with you – their networks, their insights, their skills. They confidently do so because they know you represent the future.

And niche-wise, right from the beginning when you're choosing who to interview for, consider what special interests you already have – if you have preferences, what business niche most appeals to you? In your free time, where do you enjoy focusing your attention? This is important! What excites you and gives you pleasure? If early on you can identify your particular interests, passions, fixations, compulsions, joys – if you get to know what you naturally enjoy and are attracted to, you're halfway there already. Then you'll know what you're looking for in an intern position. You're looking for something that excites you, that will give you delight in exploring.

A lot of internships, of course, aren't going to be optimal in this regard. Probably you'll have to settle for an internship that's less than ideal. Very possibly what interests you most strongly isn't as yet even a business theme. You'll need to look for any position that's even somewhat related to your key interests.

What's important is to make sure that the very next step you make is aimed in the general direction your passion wants to flow toward. And then with every new step, make sure you're still heading in your desired direction.

> *Let's pause for a few moments so that you can reflect on all this. Take time to put the book aside ... tune in to your breathing and your current feelings – and then see what thoughts, imaginations, feelings and insights come to mind when you consider the following questions:*

> > *When you have free time, where do you like to focus your attention?*

> > *In what business position can you imagine being most fulfilled in, as a future career?*

> > *Regardless of pay, what work can you envision doing with pleasure, passion, dexterity and success?*

> > *What sort of person would make a great mentor or manager during an internship?*

> > *Can you imagine openly embracing the expectation, enthusiasm and attainment of abundance?*

> > *Are you ready to express this enthusiasm when you do an intern interview?*

Choosing To Empower Yourself

My basic approach to internships is to encourage an underlying spirit of adventure and skill building, no matter what your particular intern situation might end up being. All situations will give you loads of insights, challenges, opportunities and discoveries. It all depends on your attitude toward your situation, as we've been discussing earlier in this book. If you recognize the particular levels of empowerment you individually hold in a situation, you can determine your personal outcome.

There's an old saying that goes like this: "Between the stimulus and your response lies your freedom to choose." Except in your initial choice of which companies to interview with, and which company to choose to intern with, you don't hold any power over the work environment and the people you're going to spend the summer with – that's pretty much a given. With few exceptions, you must accept that reality and make the best of it.

However, you do have great power in determining how you respond to the stimulus – to the whole work environment you drop into. I keep raising this basic point because it's so important. You can either react to a 'bad' situation with negative judgments and disappointed feelings ... or you can pause before reacting – and respond in a new way that liberates you rather than confines you. Between the stimulus and your response to that stimulus is where you can entirely transform the experience you're going to have in that company.

For instance, consider the mentor or manager who's in charge of you during your internship. I'll be talking a lot about the optimal intern mentor and you can hope to be assigned to one of these gifted and heartful teachers. In your interviews you can begin to assess who you would like to work with for a summer. But if you end up in a work situation where your manager is less than ideal, you can also positively influence this relationship.

What's key is remembering that your manager is probably still learning how to best guide an intern. If you react negatively to this person for whatever reason, justified or not, you're going to get that negativity right back at you. But if you develop the skill of not reacting but rather creatively responding to this person, you can support that manager's growth so that you both move to a better place in the relationship. There's probably going to be an equal amount of learning on the other side. Do your best to recognize that and enhance the relationship.

What I'm encouraging you to do in all your relationships is this: transform frustration into compassion and opportunity. If you're in an internship and it's less than what you wished for, so what? You have a choice. You can just indulge in feeling disappointed and upset, even angry and resentful – or you can remember that you're lucky to have been given the gift of this experience. We do tend to learn more from surviving a challenging situation than from coasting through a harmonious situation. Again, your freedom lies in seeing that you can take charge of your response, even if you can't control your situation.

What can you learn from feeling frustrated in your intern assignment? First of all, you're learning what frustrates you! You're discovering something important about yourself that can aid you for the rest of your life, and help you move consciously toward what doesn't frustrate you. Establish a commitment underneath your frustration to benefit from it.

I encourage you to regularly take notes during your internship. Write down what frustrates you. Develop lists that you can return to over and over to expand on and modify. Get down in script or print your clear preferences in life. This kind of journaling is a great tool for clarifying who you really are and what you deep-down want in life.

I've personally learned so much from bad managers and frustrating situations. One lesson has been the importance of design, of thinking through a strategy of flow ahead of time. This issue of design is fundamental for success, but so frustrating when ignored.

Observing frustration is golden! Always remember that, no matter how bad it might be, your situation is temporary – and at the end of your internship you're going to be a far better person if you endured the situation and gained new strengths and insights from making it through the ordeal.

It will benefit you to actually take the time to make detailed notes. What is it about your situation or your manager that evokes inside you the reaction of frustration or anger or resentment? What is it specifically that leaves you feeling used and unfulfilled?

Someday you'll probably be managing other people yourself – and if you've first learned these lessons yourself, you'll know how to help others through their frustration. You can look to see what happened that could have happened differently. You'll gain rare insights into what makes success possible in a company by seeing what disrupted success for you. Loads are learned from observing and striving to transcend negative situations. This is your opportunity. Whatever you do, don't walk away from it by disengaging – or worse, by quitting.

We can complain because
rose bushes have thorns,
or rejoice because
thorn bushes have roses.

Abraham Lincoln

Your Words Matter

One of the things you'll definitely begin to realize is that, at work or anywhere else, words have great power to influence the outcome of a situation. If you're paying attention while talking with someone, especially with your manager or a client or customer of the company, you'll see in action that just one off-the-cuff remark can sink a relationship. Words matter. So you've got to always consider who it is that you're talking to – consider their personality, their worries, their goals ... and also consider what you're feeling in your heart toward them.

If you're feeling disdain or judgment or impatience or some other negative emotion, your words that flow out of you are going to reflect those feelings. And once again – you do have control over your own feelings, once you gain the skills to assume that control. But I don't mean you have to be dishonest about your feelings – just the opposite. I mean you need to do the work to raise your own feelings out of chronic judgment or aggression or manipulation, into genuine feelings of acceptance, compassion and interest toward the other person.

Given that words matter, you'll probably want to spend some of your free time expanding your vocabulary. This increases your range of expression and makes it easier for you to get to the heart of the matter of whatever you're focused on. Also, practice out loud expressing what you intend to say to a person or audience. Typically, successful people rehearse and practice challenging presentations a few times before feeling ready for prime time – I certainly do.

I encourage you to practice beforehand what you will say to a manager, so you get clear for yourself what you're trying to accomplish in an upcoming communication. I'm not saying give up being spontaneous entirely. What I'm saying is exercise your ability to speak coherently with a solid vocabulary and confident presence. You might likewise benefit from speaking your piece in front of a mirror to see how you look when talking. Practice speaking while looking in the mirror until the person in the mirror (you) is fully on board with what is being said (by you).

Take three deep breaths. Now think back to a moment when you communicated either verbally or electronically and it didn't quite go as planned. Tune in to your experience of that moment and observe your breathing. Notice how you felt in that moment. Just notice.

Now, think of a time when your communication landed beautifully. Breathe slowly, and tune in to that experience.

Notice how you are feeling now. As you breathe, consider these questions:

"How good does it feel to communicate well with others?"

"What frustrations do I want to let go of now?"

"Why do I want to be an excellent communicator?"

"What might I be able to do with some new freedom to express myself?"

Pause & Reflect

~~~~~~~~~~~~~~~~~~~~~~~~~

Chapter Three

AVOIDING THE UNDERTOW
~~~~~~~~~~~~~~~~~~~~~~

Love yourself, open your heart which means
doing the work on yourself first.
Then love will follow.

Emily Morse

As a general rule, at this stage in life you're going to benefit most from situations that push your buttons, rather than ones that don't. If you learn how to consciously observe your own reactions, you're going to transform yourself. As soon as you think, "Ah, look at that, I keep reacting with the same negative feelings to that situation," you'll find that you begin to self-correct in that situation.

Often people try to avoid situations that push their buttons. But, as an intern told me: "When I'd get pushed outside my comfort zone, I'd remind myself that feeling uncomfortable was okay, that I could grow beyond my anxiety by facing it. I could become more confident and empowered if I saw the new challenge as an adventure, as something to push through rather than run away from."

You like most people probably developed most of your anxious negative reactions in early childhood. They were picked up unconsciously from the people around you. When you grow up and start seeing how those reactions interfere with your success, you'll naturally begin to change them for the better. If you end up in a 'bad' intern assignment, instead of running away you can choose to set your goal to walk out of that internship having learned to hold your own positive intent – even in challenging circumstances. Developing that skill would definitely be worth the internship in and of itself.

For instance, perhaps your manager isn't treating you with due respect. Perhaps he or she has an attitude about interns in general, that they're just in the way, they don't really have much value in the company. Okay. Turn that around and ask yourself why you're upset at not being respected. Do you actually respect yourself? And if you learn to respect yourself more during your internship, will you be able to brush off negative attitudes toward you because your own attitude toward yourself has become stronger?

The last thing you want to do is quit an internship. Don't do that or you'll be ripping yourself off. You'll be missing a golden opportunity. Instead, you need to get in there and apply your mind and your body and your emotions so that you can discover what works and what doesn't work for you. Then when you do find a good internship or a good first job or wherever you end up, you'll appreciate it that much more. You'll know what does work best – what set of people and circumstances is needed in order to come together successfully. You can't really know that unless you know the other side of it. This is similar to 'not knowing success until you know failure.'

> *When you look back over your life thus far, what comes to mind related to disempowering situations you got stuck in – and what did you learned from those kinds of situations?*

> *This is a big question, so take time to see if in your own past, you've already learned a great deal from difficult people and environments. And through this reflection, see if you can learn something new from those challenging times.*

You cannot control everything
that is coming at you
but you can control
how you react.

Bryan Tracy

Moving Beyond Your Parents

Part of the college experience and also the internship process is about letting go of your parents as your primary influence in your life, and focusing on new mentors whom you trust to influence your future. This broadens your horizons. To do this, it's wise to begin by looking back at who your parents really are – what their formative life experiences were even before you were born. In moving through this process, you'll gain a new perspective and some needed identity-defining distance. This will enable you to then consciously choose which qualities of theirs you want to hold on to, and which qualities you want to actively let go of and move beyond.

Let me share with you how this reflective process works, by going through the process here myself. By the way, it also helps to write this biographical information down if you feel motivated and have the time. In my case I was born in Rhode Island but my dad was born in Palestine in the city of Nazareth in the early 1930s. His dad was not a very good man. He was a schoolteacher who liked alcohol and gambling, and at times he lacked compassion.

My dad learned literally to be the opposite of his dad through watching his father's mistreatment of his mom and family. Today, in his late 80s, he doesn't touch alcohol, doesn't gamble, and has always been very kind. He was also a hard worker before retiring. The educational system in Palestine was very rough, you had to study day and night to succeed – which is what my dad did. He was always the top of his class because he worked so hard. But he also enjoyed himself, he loved playing table tennis and marbles – and he was (and still is) an outstanding Arabic poet.

Then very suddenly in 1948 his family left Palestine, because of the situation with the founding of Israel. He went to study at the University of Damascus in Syria and spent seven years studying in the French system to become a medical doctor. It was extremely competitive. If you failed at any point, you were done. In reflection, I can see that my own hard-working study habits in school reflected my dad's earlier study habits. I'm thankful for inheriting his drive to focus and work so intently – but also I've learned not to be so single-minded that I miss out on most of the rest of life. Through those systems he didn't gain much formal knowledge outside of medicine.

I remember how, when I was at Princeton, I told my dad about all the new things I was doing on campus – and he got very upset. He assumed that I'd be studying all the time. His formula for success was simply to work harder than everyone else. And this was literally all the advice I got from my parents when I went to Princeton. But it wasn't useful for dealing with all my emotional struggles at the time. That's why I looked to find someone else to talk to, like a professional counselor – someone in the know about my new situations and challenges.

> *What about your relationship with your father or father figure – what was your father's life story, and how did it influence how he brought you up? Is he still your primary influence, or have you found someone on campus you can talk openly with and learn new life or survival skills?*
>
> *Also, are you perhaps looking for a mentor during your internship who can be of help to you in ways your father perhaps isn't? Take a few moments to see what comes to mind in this regard.*

And then there's your mother or mother figure – what was her story, and how did she influence your current attitudes and assumptions about work and life? My mom was born in the mid-40s in Palestine, in a city called Jaffa. She was very young when her family left Palestine in 1948. Her family, like my father's, were civilians who chose not to engage in the war as fighters – so they left and relocated in Damascus.

My mom was from a fairly well-to-do family, well-known in Palestine. She went to school in Damascus and then met my dad when she was 17. They got married after just two months of courting, and she was a mother a year later. That's how they did things back in the early '60s in Arab-speaking southwest Asia. Having kids and raising a loving family was my mom's life plan, and she has succeeded with that goal in spades.

Meanwhile my dad had become a medical doctor and was offered an opportunity to come to America to work. I was born a few years after they arrived in the northeast U.S. I can imagine how hard that must have been for my mom, suddenly thrown into a new culture half-way around the world at age 18 with a family to raise and no college education or even much English. She suddenly lost her extended family circle – she in fact lost everything but her husband and her budding family. So of course she wouldn't be able to imagine, let alone advise on, what I was going through at a fancy American university decades later.

Another sudden jolt struck our family in 1975, when after just having moved back to Lebanon two years before, civil war broke out. Looking back, I can see how rough that whole situation was for my parents – and of course for me too. I couldn't control anything that was happening around me, all the grenades and bullets and the whole deal, right there in front of my six-year-old eyes. I remember a man coming running into our building bleeding with shrapnel in his shoulder. My dad went to work taking out the metal shards. This happened one morning on an otherwise sunny beautiful day.

We were living in a building that my mother's family owned. Almost all of its six floors housed various members of her family. Before the war started, it had been truly wonderful to run around playing with all my cousins in the building, feeling that comforting sense of our extended family all under one roof. My mother must have been so relieved to be back home close to her parents and able to socialize with everybody she'd grown up with.

But then the civil war started and everything rapidly changed for the worse. There was real danger everywhere around us. One night, we ended up sleeping in the basement for fear of bombs overhead. I remember falling asleep expecting a bomb to hit our building and the whole building crushing down on us – instant death. For a six-year-old, that was a terrible final image to have before sleeping.

In college, I was able to understand a lot about my mother and father by reflecting on their lives. At Princeton I started this reflective process, but I was also caught up in rebellious feelings that clouded my perception of them at the time. However, I could certainly understand their intense feelings about almost worshipping peace. From Lebanon we had moved to Jordan to wait out the war – but then in a couple of months we were moving again, back to America, back to the biggest little state in the union: Rhode Island. By age nine I had lived in five different homes in three countries.

I became more and more like my dad, perhaps because of my early-childhood war traumas. I developed a manic drive in my studies and athletics to do as well as I possibly could. That drive is what got me into Princeton. In fact I still have it and deeply value it. In whatever I'm doing, I want to do my very best. But I also do everything I can to regularly turn off that chronic push, because it's the sort of mental and emotional programming that leads to chronic stress and zero time for fun.

You'll perhaps discover in reflection that what you learned unconsciously in childhood is a mixed blessing that needs conscious regulation. Back at Princeton, I really had nothing else but my studies to hold on to. There was almost no real Arab voice or presence on campus, and supporting the Palestinian side of debates wasn't considered politically correct on campus back in the late '80s. Finding any common inherited ground was very hard for me and it also wasn't my raison d'être. So on campus I just kept my mouth shut, watched, and got along.

Family religious orientation is also something to reflect on in college as you explore a perhaps wider range of beliefs and theologies, or choose to put aside such things. I was brought up in the Orthodox Church, which was a minority religion and almost non-existent at Princeton. I'd participated with my family in a small Arab community in Rhode Island and the Orthodox church there. They're good people, but during and after Princeton I didn't go to church much anymore. Traditional religion just didn't really speak to me and my Arab identity wasn't so important to me either.

So – with all that convoluted family background, I found myself at Princeton, and just had to get by as best I could. Probably you had a smoother family history than I did, I certainly hope so. I recognize that the struggles of my parents and my early childhood were difficult, but I value them highly because they did form me. I am who I am partly because of those struggles. It's deeply important for a healthy personality to accept the past rather than live in denial.

But at the same time, perpetuating ingrained negative attitudes and emotional constrictions resulting from long-gone traumatic experiences is counterproductive. For my kids, my goal has been to provide a sense of stability that I had lacked. We committed for instance to live in the same house in Chicago rather than move, no matter how high or low our fortunes go. There's a special inner quality a child develops when allowed to grow up immersed in a stable neighborhood community. Today I have no intention of moving my family just because a career opportunity might open up somewhere else.

> *To what extent did your own family's trials and tribulations, as well as their good times and successes, determine who you are now? Specifically, when you look back, how much of your personality, your worries, your hopes and aspirations are founded upon the beliefs and feelings, attitudes and life history of your mother or other parental figure?*
>
> *Take a few moments to consider if you feel acceptance toward your parents and your family history – or are you still caught up in some negative feelings? Also, are you feeling in rebellion against your upbringing, or do you feel free of all that?*

Selective Focus Is Everything

You only have so much focal attention to spend each day of your life. And at any given moment you can only focus on one particular thing or thought. The choices you make about what to focus on each new moment are perhaps the most important choices you make. In my case for instance, if I actively choose to put my time and effort toward the Palestinian cause, where realistically I'll have minimal impact on the situation, I'll have to give up focusing on other things where I might have a much more meaningful and lasting impact. Each of us must continually determine how to best spend our personal power and focal attention.

There's definitely a sober responsibility that each of us hopefully learns to assume as we grow up regarding what's most important to us – and therefore where we choose to focus our power of attention. During college you're in the process of deciding what your calling is in life. Where do you want truly to make a difference? How do you want to see yourself and how do you not want to be seen? For me, I choose to be helpful to as many people as possible in my community, rather than getting overly caught up in distant struggles.

Because time and energy are limited, where you spend it is always a choice. For my parents, who are by nature very peaceful and welcoming and kind to everybody, it's been hard for them to leave their homeland and watch its history unfold as it has. I speak of the Palestinian struggle here because that's my background. You have yours to contend with. If you're an African American, maybe you confront the abhorrent crime of slavery perpetuated for hundreds of years in the "land of the free." If you're Asian American, perhaps you struggle with unwarranted violence against your community. You can fill in the blank with whatever personal political or ethnic challenge you deal with.

What my father found to be most fulfilling to focus his attention upon was delivering babies – he definitely found his niche, he delivered over ten thousand babies. And on his days off, he did volunteer work at a health center providing care to those in need. Even when he was 75, he still was delivering babies. That's my dad! Did your father provide you with a positive work ethic mixing duty and pleasure, good income and community service?

I also want to mention my mom. She ran our household and took primary responsibility for four children. She also went out and got her Associates Degree, demonstrating for the rest of our family that women can lead a household, and also in her case, provide community service at the local hospital and her church. To this day, she is a powerful leader in the church community. I learned so much from her example.

In college I began learning how to separate myself from limiting attitudes and assumptions, where that was necessary for my own freedom of choice. I then went into the business world with my ups and downs, but through lots of non-traditional training and development I managed to eventually support and later create successful companies. While in college, my philosophy of life built on my family background and evolved from there. It's based on honoring integrity while also enjoying each moment, looking constantly for fresh opportunity, and putting people before profits. Like my parents, I strive to be as kind and helpful to others as I can. And I've managed to be a part of and found companies that strive toward win-win relationships. What philosophy of life and work are you developing step by step?

I've focused my talents and energies in directions that felt best for me, my family, my alumni and colleagues and broader community. But I'm not here to tell you what's most important to focus on. How you choose to spend your energy and creativity is entirely up to you. What I'm recommending is that before an internship, and certainly before you graduate and enter the business world, take time to get to know yourself better in terms of the impact of your childhood on your present attitudes, mood swings, passions and intentions.

If you focus attention in these directions in college, and bring closure to them, you'll be free to focus on what's most important to you as you start your career.

> *If you look back, and also keep an eye on your future, what would you say are the three main positive qualities you learned early on from your parents that you want to emulate in your intern position and as you move beyond college into the business world?*

> *Also – where do you prefer to focus your power of attention in the present moment? What gives you the most pleasure to focus on? What are your natural inclinations when it comes to paying attention?*

Pause & Reflect

~~~~~~~~~~~~~~~~~~~~~~~~

Chapter Four

READY WITH AN EVEN KEEL

~~~~~~~~~~~~~~~~~~~~~~

*Gratitude is not only
the greatest of virtues,
it's the parent of all the others.*

Marcus Tullius Cicero

The whole notion of emotional intelligence is of course really important for success in your career, but it's a dimension of education minimally focused on in college. This is unfortunate because it's going to make loads of difference when you get your internship and your first job. If you're a bit of a mess emotionally like I was, no matter how smart you are, you're going to run into a lot of problems in the workplace. So let's talk a bit about this thing called emotional intelligence – which means how well you understand and manage your own inner feelings.

When I was in college I didn't know anything at all about emotional intelligence. I was the opposite of balanced, of steering my way through life's emotional storms with an even keel. Instead I would experience incredible highs when things went well, but then swing down into terrible lows when things didn't go well. Whether it was academic, social, sports, or just some random thing, I could feel super bright or dangerously low without any control over the swings. In fact, those radical swings were my normal.

What did I do to escape the lows? I guess I did what most students around me did – I just wallowed in my mood unable to accomplish anything, or I drank alcohol in excess, or maybe went off campus to get away for a while. Also, as I mentioned, I found the resource of an on-campus therapist who helped me a lot to comprehend my mood swings.

Also, when in a high mood I'd try to keep it going and stay in the excitement, knowing it was ephemeral but wanting to sustain it as long as possible – and even build on it, even though I knew at some point it would slip away. Even when I felt elated, there was a lurking apprehension underlying the elation. There was also a nagging anxiety about being strong and capable intellectually while knowing I was weak and a mess emotionally.

Ah, if only I'd known back then what I know now about emotional intelligence! For instance, we don't have to be victims of our mood swings – we can step by step learn to manage our feelings so that we're more even-keeled. Some of this learning comes only with experience as the years go by and we naturally grow more mature. But even in college, you can actively accelerate this process. That's what self-reflection is all about – observing your mood swings and acquiring emotional skills that let you take charge of your feelings, rather than being pushed around by them.

It surely helps to realize you're not the only one struggling with your feelings in college – pretty much everyone on campus is, in their own way. The progression from family life back home into adult life on your own is typically not easy. You're having to shift beyond the mindset and emotional atmosphere you were born into and advance into a more autonomous stance in life. You must graduate from your support group back home and must somehow build a new support group out in the world.

There are two steps to developing mature emotional skills. The first is learning to observe, understand and modify your existing emotional reactions to various different situations. The second is establishing a new set of conscious responses with your friends. Developing honest compassionate friendships in college is very important – because a true friend by definition is someone who accepts you for who you are, someone who believes in your narrative.

Even with the best of parents, community and circumstances, we experience hurt feelings, disappointments and emotional challenges in childhood. For some, these incidents were like mini-PTSD experiences that no one else realized were traumatic for us. When we arrive in college we need to begin acknowledging our constrained emotions, reflexive anxieties, and lurking depressions. It's time to do an introspective review, so that we can then move through the inner process of advancing beyond all our childhood contractions.

The universal experience of coming of age and getting blasted with a surge of hormones is in itself seriously disruptive emotionally. Your body is going through a series of maturations that you must somehow cope with and make your own. This is always an uphill battle. The most important thing is to recognize what's happening and be patient with yourself, even when you're caught up in wild mood upswings and downswings. Perhaps most important of all is not to take it all too seriously.

As you watch yourself and your feelings, you'll notice that there are some emotions you habitually block and reject and otherwise try to deny. Emotional intelligence holds front-and-center the importance of learning to accept all of your feelings, not just the good ones. Otherwise, when you repress them, they're liable to sneak up on you and disrupt your life.

Many parents are afraid of their own anger, for instance, and so their children grow up with this same habitual blockage. Or perhaps crying was frowned upon, or expressing worries and fears. Even 'good' feelings like excitement, joy, passion, hope and love itself can be discouraged or even punished when expressed in a household. Your job in college and beyond is to notice what emotions you tend to block or reject or feel afraid to express – and begin to welcome them into your full emotional repertoire.

There are in fact no bad emotions – otherwise we wouldn't have evolved with them. Every emotion has its time and place, and also its successful form of expression. To chronically reject a feeling will ultimately leave you feeling emotionally out of touch, because you're denying yourself your full expression. Conversely, as you begin to accept and express a forbidden or feared emotion, you'll gain newfound strength and resilience that will serve you well. You'll be able to respond appropriately to any situation you might find yourself engaged in.

To look a bit deeper into all this, you might want to pause now and ask yourself a few questions. Remember that your emotions are expressed through your breathing, so stay aware of your breathing as you reflect on the following questions:

What feelings do you usually block from expression?

What emotions are you afraid to get caught feeling?

Are you good at hiding and faking your true inner feelings?

What do you do when you find yourself feeling anxious?

How do you deal with feeling depressed and hopeless?

What are you most deathly afraid of?

Do you tend to inhibit feelings of joy and pleasure?

When you imagine yourself arriving for your first day of work as an intern, what feelings do you think will dominate your emotional presence?

When you observe your breathing right now, what feelings do you find under pressure inside you?

How would you rate your own emotional intelligence?

Pause & Reflect

~~~~~~~~~~~~~~~~~~~~~~~~~

Aiming For Spiritual Autonomy

Another key element of a successful college life has to do with your inherited religious upbringing. Regardless of your family's theological alignment or independence from any particular religious tradition, you absorbed this heritage and bias from a very early age onward. Your language itself was imbued with the concepts and beliefs, laws and aspirations of your religious or secular environment as a child.

And then comes college, where you step beyond that environment into a more neutral and diversified spiritual atmosphere, where students and teachers carry a whole host of different religious beliefs and traditions. Your job as you mature will be to explore what you yourself choose to believe or let go of believing at deeper spiritual levels of engagement.

Because you're not ever going to find anyone out in the world who believes exactly what you were brought up to believe, tolerance is the obvious key word when you get to college. You want to be accepted just as you are – and you're going to need to learn how to accept people with seriously-different beliefs than you espouse. And certainly, when you land suddenly in a work environment as an intern, you're going to be expected to keep your religious preferences to yourself and not in any way push your beliefs on other people in your company.

So again – be prepared to do some soul-searching before you intern! Perhaps you came from a strict religious background loaded with harsh judgments of all people who didn't believe the same as your community. Perhaps you were brought up with no religious affiliation at all or inside a minority religious group. You'll find that tolerance is always the optimum stance. Our society was built on religious freedom for a purpose. Tolerance helps us be inclusive, fair and open-minded. And achieving this personal stance can sometimes be a challenge.

Aiming toward this goal, you might begin to observe how you react or respond when encountering people who express different beliefs and theologies than your own. Do you feel threatened by them? Do you feel the impulse to preach at them and try to make them believe what you do? In getting to know yourself better, this level of self-reflection is critical. If you don't develop your ability to be tolerant and accepting, you're going to run into serious trouble on the job.

Achieving spiritual autonomy means that you've grown up to where you're choosing what you prefer spiritually, rather than just blindly believing what you were taught in childhood to believe about life. When you achieve spiritual autonomy, you are no longer threatened by people with different beliefs than you. You stand on your own two feet spiritually and allow other people to do the same. If someone different than you talks about what they believe, or even tries to convert you, you don't have to react. You're secure in your own beliefs. You're free!

This will be especially important in your intern work when talking with your manager, your colleagues and your clients. Of course they're different than you – that's how the world is. And in the workplace it's assumed that you've reached a level of spiritual autonomy where you live and let live. You do your work knowing that religious tolerance is the name of the game. You feel secure enough in your own faith that you aren't threatened or bothered when relating with people of divergent faiths.

I was brought up as an Orthodox Christian. That was my spiritual identity and basically still is today. Do you have a spiritual identity? What do you call yourself, if anything? Do you belong to a religious tradition that you adhere to? Is this solid or in flux? Getting to know yourself means bringing this sense of religious or philosophical identity up to the surface of your reflective mind, to where you feel clear and positive about what you truly value in life.

College encourages this level of self-exploration. You discover all sorts of divergent belief systems in the world and begin to decide which if any seem to fit how you naturally see the world. This is an ongoing evolution throughout life. Admitting that you're still openly exploring your own spiritual identity is a vital step into maturity.

> *Life is a process.*
> *Improve the quality of the process*
> *and you improve the quality of life itself.*
>
> **Moishe Feldenkrais**

Universal Values And Virtues

Another quite effective way of approaching this whole issue of politics, religion and work is to focus not on how you're different from the people around you, but rather on what is universal to human spiritual and ethical levels of relating. The business world, for instance, is full of people from all political views and religious traditions – but the business world also universally embraces certain values, virtues and aspirations. If you focus on the beliefs that hold us all together, you can readily express political and religious tolerance.

It's now well-documented in anthropology that for thousands of years almost all human civilizations around the world have held certain values and virtues in common. There's a fairly universal sense of right and wrong, good and bad, enriching and demeaning behavior. For instance, the virtues of being honest and fair are held in highest regard around the world. Whatever your background might be, in the workplace the belief in these values is, generally speaking, universal. Companies and countries that erode positive values tend to flounder in the end.

If you want to succeed in your internship, there are definite values and virtues that will help empower you. Reflecting on these, and choosing to consciously uphold them in your first job, can be the most important thing you do. As examples, you'll find that regularly expressing empathy, honesty, cooperation and patience are virtues that will help you succeed in the workplace. So are the qualities of diligence, authenticity, enthusiasm and integrity. It's also of value to be grateful, thoughtful and light-hearted – plus you'll usually be rewarded for having self-control and being emotionally balanced.

In your upbringing you might have been rewarded for nurturing these values and virtues – but you also might have grown up in a family where they were not adhered to. Perhaps your parents thought it was okay to cheat here and there, to be dishonest at times, and to fixate on hateful or spiteful feelings. Maybe getting away with doing shoddy work was okay. Maybe your mom lacked enthusiasm for work, or your dad got stuck in chronic negative judgments.

If so, you've got some important inner work to do if you want to get along and be respected and valued at work. Rest assured that everyone tends to have their weak points on this virtues front. We all have room to improve our deeper spiritual and philosophical stance so that we can truly shine at work (and in other areas of our lives). What's important is getting to know and fully owning the values and virtues that enhance business success. Exploring how your own life resonates with these values is a highly useful endeavor.

And throughout, do keep in mind that the universal virtues found in the business place aren't just ideas. They are heartful whole-body feelings. Honesty for instance isn't just a cold philosophical notion. Like your spiritual presence, your moral presence *is* you – it's your identity. And best of all, this identity can evolve. You can nurture your sense of moral integrity – you're not just born with it or without it.

Also, begin to observe other people in this regard. Are they trustworthy? Are they compassionate? Do they deal with you fairly? What are their values, and how well do they live up to them? Then turn this around and begin to observe yourself.

To help you reflect in this direction, here is a list of virtues that seem to resonate within all enduring societies, philosophies, and religions. I recommend that you pause once a week and read down this list. See how you currently feel toward each one. Doing this self-reflection will help you evolve step by step to where you can enter any workplace and do well in your dealings.

> *To move through this process, it helps to first get in touch with your breathing, which can serve as an internal barometer revealing how each term strikes you. Spend a few breaths on each virtue and observe how your mind and feelings respond to the term:*
>
> *... empathy*
>
> *... cooperation*
>
> *... forgiveness*
>
> *... honesty*
>
> *... simplicity*
>
> *... patience*
>
> *... diligence*
>
> *... authenticity*
>
> *... acceptance*
>
> *... enthusiasm*
>
> *... gratitude*
>
> *... humor*

... integrity

... equanimity

... generosity

... brightness

... self-esteem

... reverence

... thoughtfulness

... wisdom

... excellence

... trustworthiness

... fairness

... self-control

... joy

To end this reflection, you might want to just relax and consider again how you feel about the core human qualities. Do you in fact want to be virtuous, meaning living a life based on positive values and intentions? Or in truth, do you prefer to just get out there and play by whatever rules and maneuvers will bring in the most profit and power?

Happiness is the spiritual experience
of living every minute
with love, grace, and gratitude.

Denis Waitley

Something To Hold On To

When you get accepted into an internship, you're perhaps going to feel a bit over your head because the whole situation is going to be new to you. You won't really know what to expect, what working with others will be like, or how you're going to perform in a new environment. In any such situation, you're going to need an inner sense of solidity and confidence to get you through. Where are you going to find this inner feeling of groundedness? A lot of what we've been talking about thus far relates to this question. Now let's look even a bit deeper.

The world of business is too often seen as a heartless competitive arena where your deeper spiritual and philosophical leanings don't really matter, or worse, get in the way of succeeding. But in my business life I've found just the opposite to be true. People without a deep spiritual or philosophical grounding don't tend to do well in business in the long run. Having no substance deep-down can cause one's whole situation to unravel. But people with a solid spiritual foundation tend to flourish. When the going gets tough, being able to tap into a deep well of wisdom, truth and principles can be a lifesaver.

This solid spiritual foundation is found within, not externally. We all need acceptance and love, but when we rely only on the outside world for these feelings, we can flounder. If we don't first love and accept our own selves, if we don't feel some inner connection with a higher power, a deeper wisdom, an ultimate universal goodness and inner guide, our life will end up feeling empty and pointless. So I encourage you to look inward for your primary ballast, for your sense of confidence and groundedness.

Regardless of whether you're Christian or Hindu, agnostic or atheist, pantheist or no formal label, what matters is setting time aside regularly to pause and look inward. Find out who you really are beyond your superficial personality traits. Make the quiet contemplative move of focusing inward, with your thoughts momentarily quiet. Discover your core spiritual substratum so that you feel some trustworthy solid ground to stand on in life.

It's a cliché to talk about listening to your inner voice, but this is a primal key to gaining self-knowledge, autonomy, confidence, wisdom, purpose and all the rest. I tried to find acceptance and love externally by joining the wrestling team at Princeton and an Eating Club and several other organizations. Though each was a valuable experience that helped, they didn't relieve me of my inner sense of emptiness, of not belonging anywhere. Only through inner soul-searching did I slowly begin to realize that it was my relationship with my own deeper self that held the power to relieve my existential suffering. Only as I learned how to shift my focus inward did I begin to feel like my true self, loved and accepted by me – something authentic and enduring that I could confidently hold on to.

Of course it's also important to engage with the world around you, to discover how you fit into the social and work world. For instance when I did some catering work on campus and delivered pizzas for the student pizza agency, I gained a fresh perspective on how I relate with other people. Life is a paradox because we must look inward, and at the same time, engage outwardly in order to feel truly human. So it's vital to consciously do both – retreat and reflect on who you really are, and also go out and commit, engage, and learn from your social mistakes and adventures.

So much of college life these days is shifting from in-person relating to digital interactions. There's a latent danger in this on several levels, because it's far too easy to lose awareness of our physical whole-body presence while relating online. The digital reality is devoid of a crucial dimension – our biological physicality. But really, who are we without our bodily presence? Consider that when you get to your intern position, they're not just looking to deal with you as a dissociated well-programmed brain. They're looking to see who you are as a living organism, a physical and emotional presence.

To be blunt, we're becoming very much a disembodied society. For many of us, we do most of our daily work with our minds and very little actual work with our whole bodies. But let's always remember that each of our emotions requires a body in order to be felt! We become greatly reduced as human beings if we spend most of our lives fixated above our necks. What are we going to do if we suddenly fall in love, or are required to engage as whole human beings in the workplace? With this in mind, it's clear that we need to make a conscious effort to become embodied again. We need to get physical and re-establish our heart feelings as central.

What can you do to drop down into your body? First of all, Train yourself to consciously put aside your thoughts and shift your focus toward the ongoing experience of your whole body. Do this often each new day – pause from your mental fixations for ten breaths every half hour and tune in to the actual physical sensations and emotions flowing through your body. For instance when you're walking from class to class, tune in to your breathing and whole-body presence rather than staying fixated on thoughts about the past and the future.

Another good way to shift often into whole-body presence is to take up a casual sport – toss a Frisbee with friends, go jogging or enjoy some other physical exercise on a daily basis. And in everything you do, make focusing on your ongoing breath sensations a constant habit (that's what mindfulness is all about). Take time to enjoy all the muscular and sensory pleasures of your physical presence – delight in movement!

> *Right now, if you want to, see what experience comes to you if you put this book aside after reading this paragraph ... close your eyes ... tune in to the sensation of the air flowing effortlessly in and out through your nose ... and as you count ten breaths going by, be open to a new experience!*

Pause & Look Inward

~~~~~~~~~~~~~~~~~~~~~~~~~~~~~~

Chapter Five

BEING AUTHENTIC
~~~~~~~~~~~~~~~~~~

*Don't pretend to be
someone you're not.*

Oprah Winfrey

Long before you do your first interview for an intern position, you'll want to start reflecting on how to master the interview process. All too often, students carry quite warped notions about what it's like to enter the competition for good internships. Most students don't take adequate time to prepare themselves for the interview experience. In the following discussions we'll look at not only the challenge of finding a good internship, but also the value of preparing yourself for that search.

Organic Networking

Part of this preparation process involves successful networking – but the value and process of networking has recently been hyped a bit. Kids in high school are being told to start networking immediately for their future success. But as you probably already know, it's obnoxious to meet with people in college who're relating with you just to further their future connections in the workplace.

Because of this over-hype, I feel that it's wise to reframe networking. For me, successful networking means two people with common interests wanting to keep in touch as friends and perhaps assist each other where possible later on in life.

From this perspective, networking in college begins not by going out to connect with people who might do something for you in the future, but rather by working to develop yourself so that you have something of value to offer other people. Make yourself interesting to be around by expanding things like your vocabulary, your travels, your reading list, your knowledge of interesting technology or research, or perhaps your ability to code, play a musical instrument, or discuss philosophy. When you become rich in experience and knowledge, people will naturally want to stay in touch with you.

Being likable is a very important trait to develop. Some people are born more extroverted while others are more introverted – but being likable isn't innate. You can purposefully brighten your presence so that others want to be with you. You might want to observe your relating habits in various situations and see how often you are mostly self-fixated as opposed to focused on others.

It's always rewarding when you take time to find out what other people are feeling and doing. You might focus specifically on learning how to become a highly-attentive listener – and decide to open your heart more fully and genuinely care about others. Relating is all about taking the time to focus on another person. If you don't learn to do this, your networking ability is going to remain stunted.

Being likeable starts with learning to like your own self. If you were brought up to constantly judge yourself as not quite adequate, you're going to project that image out into the world, and people will see you in that uninspiring way too. Looking inward and developing the ability to accept and love yourself, just as you are, is actually a primary precursor of your future success in networking.

Another sometimes-helpful note on relating: when you're talking with someone, begin to notice if you're mostly fixated up in your head, being quite clever with ideas and perhaps dominating a conversation – or if you're staying aware of your breathing and your heart feelings so that you come across as warm and enjoyable to be with. The subtle process of sharing your feelings is what generates friendship, and networking emerges organically from when you nurture that effortless friendship bond.

That said, of course get out and practice networking while still in college. Personal connections can unexpectedly lead to such things as finding a great summer job. So do actively go out and network to get the intern position you want most – and also make the effort to stay in touch with those folks who help you get there. Just don't make 'networking for networking's sake' a top priority in college.

Keep in mind that networking means not only using connections to get ahead. Networking also means giving of yourself – having something to offer and regularly offering it as a gift, not as a calculated exchange. Be open and friendly. Listen and contribute to others. Be helpful without expecting any return. And yes, trust that what goes around will come around – it definitely does.

Creating Time To Care

I think perhaps the best networking you can do is staying in touch with people with whom you've gone through something significant. Your roommates, teammates, bandmates or fellow majors are ideal. Start with people who you're naturally drawn to, who you resonate with and share similar interests. Purposefully nurture your ability to feel genuine compassion for them. Let your heart expand and let your circle of friends expand. Then watch your network expand effortlessly. For instance, today many of my wife's friends are my friends too. Through her we have something in common that we can perhaps build upon. And remember to be consistent. Don't go to people only when you need something. You're not really building a valuable relationship if you only call, text or email someone when you are in need. It's important to be actively giving over time, regardless of need.

Like I said before, my basic advice on career networking is to be authentically interested in others. Be sure when communicating to think about what's in the other person's best interest. Set aside a certain amount of time each day when you pause and tune in to your heart and think of people you might be able to support or make a difference in their career.

Maybe send a text or an email just to stay in touch and demonstrate interest. Just ... be caring. Choose to practice giving without expecting anything in return. I assure you, the returns will be forthcoming – and often in entirely unexpected ways.

Nothing ventured, nothing gained, and nothing still remains. You gotta do something to gain something – just don't expect it to be linear. I remember back at Princeton when the academic workload was so heavy it seemed like I didn't have any free time to focus loving attention on being there for other people. College can be a nonstop self-fixated experience, to say the least. And that's a major difficulty if you also want to develop your capacity to network and 'be there' for others.

Time is a limited resource – and what do you do with limited resources? You prioritize. You make the most out of the time you have each day, by spending your time focused on what's most important to you. You need to consciously plan how you're going to use your limited time, attention and energy. Pause and put yourself in your own future shoes, and envision how you intend to walk through your day five years from now, ten, fifteen, twenty years in the future. And as you live through today, make clear decisions about what's most important in order to create the future you envision – and implement those decisions rigorously.

From time to time I keep a journal. When I look back through that journal, I'm often shocked at what's in there. It's like I am reading about someone else's life. Did I actually choose to spend my time as I did back then – was I conscious, or just drifting with whatever came my way? Why did I focus my attention where I did? What was I thinking? The value for me of this practice is having another avenue for self-reflection and knowing myself, based on actual events rather than vague memories. I recommend you try journaling yourself. Establish the daily discipline of writing down what you actually did, thought and experienced that day. Then a week later, a month or a year later, go back and re-read your journal. You will gain new insights into how you can more intentionally manage your time.

Perhaps a counterintuitive insight to wise time management is found in choosing to let go of the whole concept that time is limited, even though it is. Learning to let it go can be freeing. What if time is just the steady almost eternal spinning of our planet? It's not necessarily a scarce factor in life. It's just there for us to participate in. Every new moment is a free gift to us, and ultimately we have the freedom to do whatever we want with each new moment. But here's the crucial thing – we only have that freedom if we realize we do. We must consciously pause and choose in each moment what's most important to focus on.

Keeping a journal of what's going on
in your life is a good way to help you
distill what's important and what's not.

Martina Navratilova

The Optimal Applicant

When you interview for a job of any kind, you are also actively networking if you choose to make it that. And the same rules apply. Don't be totally self-centered. Show interest in who the interviewer is. Get in tune with how they feel and what interests them. They're having an experience while talking with you too. So be concerned about whether they're enjoying the interview process.

Through being a good listener and asking interesting questions about them, you're showing the interviewer that you care about the experience they're having. That right there will set you apart. And also remember that you need to evaluate the company during the interview. As one intern put it, "I realized that an interview is also a way for me to 'interview' the firm to see if they'd be a good fit for me."

You can make these in-action evaluations and exchanges best either in person, or perhaps through video call. Whenever possible, do go beyond just applying online for an internship. Instead, whenever you can, make meaningful face-to-face contacts with companies. Make full use of networking through people you know. When you apply online you're going up against thousands of similar resumes. In reality, few positions in a company are filled through a random resume showing up on someone's computer screen. Things happen mostly through referrals, through someone being recommended by someone close to the company – that's just how it goes. Networking becomes very important when you're reaching out into the business world for work.

Now, one way or another you have set up an interview regarding an internship that interests you. What's going to happen in that interview? When I'm interviewing a student for an internship, I love to meet someone who isn't totally self-absorbed, someone who takes some interest in me. I'm looking for someone who's going to be proactive and an emotional plus in the workplace – and self-absorbed people usually don't meet those goals.

I hired two interns during the winter months last year and my decisions were based primarily on how they reached out in my direction. For instance, one of them sent me an email that was so thoughtful and considerate, genuine and open-hearted that I literally stopped everything and contacted her right back. Her email made her likable immediately.

What was she doing? She was being authentic. I could tell she felt confident inside her own skin, and that she was looking to contribute. I could feel her presence emotionally just in the words she'd used to reach out to me. She was offering genuine emotional warmth and an eagerness to share. She made me want to hire her by virtue of her wanting to be of service to me and my company.

Also – she wasn't bragging to me about all the great things she can do. She wasn't overwhelming me with nonstop self-promotion. She was drawing parallels between her college experience as an athlete and mine. As a result, she naturally connected – and she became someone I'd recommend even if I didn't hire her myself. That's the best flow, that's how true networking flows: humans working together in a win-win supportive game with both parties giving and taking equally.

The key is to keep company
only with people who uplift you,
whose presence calls forth your best.

Epictetus

True Sales Skills

In an intern interview or email, or in whatever way you interact, you're selling yourself. But selling isn't just a rote technique that you read about and try to replicate in action. Selling anything, including your unique value for an intern position, is optimally an authentic expression of feeling connected to others and clearly demonstrating interest. It's more than "I'm going to do something for you." That's not a winning long-term strategy. In life, it's more like knowing how to ask questions in order to see what the other person really needs and is looking for.

Put simply – if you can fulfill that need for them at a reasonable cost, then you have a sale. So take time to find out what the interviewer needs in an intern. Ask questions. If you honestly have what they're looking for, present that – and you might have a position. You might have a sale.

Primarily, you want to come from a posture of service, of caring, and this always involves being genuinely curious about the other person. Ask questions that provide an opportunity for them to open up about themselves. Make inquiries that widen the discussion rather than narrow it down. Avoid questions that can be answered with a yes or no. Keep the conversation expanding. If things line up with what you're offering, great. Together, over time, the two of you can perhaps build something real and of mutual value.

Also, if you're genuinely interested in people, you're going to remember facts you learn about them for future discussions. I encourage you to take notes after each conversation. Make the effort to memorize details about your interviewer's life that you learned in the conversation. Making this concerted effort to remember details shows that you're authentically caring. Ultimately, as we're seeing, caring is a concerted choice that you make – to invest your valuable time and effort in expanding the relationship, and perhaps nurturing a future friendship or resource.

But this impulse to remember things about people needs to come from the heart, not from manipulative intentions of the plotting mind. If you're being phony, you'll be found out. That's why it's so important to know yourself, and never present yourself as something you are not. Generally as an intern applicant, you're adequately qualified – that's not usually the issue. If they wanted experienced people they wouldn't be talking to interns. The issue is whether you're going to fit into the company and contribute not just performance-wise but community-wise as well.

Your potential contribution will be obvious if you are truly interested, if you're a good listener and confident in your skills. If you're a curious and caring person, you're probably going to be among the top of the list.

Think back to the most recent time you wrote an application for a position you really wanted – this was probably your application to get into a college of your choice. If you did your best with that application, you most likely sought out teachers and so forth to write recommendations for you. That was perhaps your first taste of networking! If you established significant positive relationships with your teachers, they then gave you good reviews – and organic networking will have worked for you.

For better or for worse, you actively sold yourself to colleges. But also remember that at the same time, they were selling themselves to you. In a similar vein, an interviewer will be selling a potential intern on the opportunity of working within their company for a set period of time. Such interviews are always a bidirectional sales situation.

So be sure to allow ample time and space for interviewers to talk about and promote their company. You're both a consumer and a product in this regard. You're a consumer looking at companies, and you're a product of your particular high school and college looking to be 'bought' for a trial period called an internship. When your college sold you on it, and you sold yourself on them, at that moment there was a good fit and a deal was made. Probably it was the biggest sales transaction you'd ever made in your life to that point – without you even realizing it.

Fast forward. You're now in college and you have to sell yourself again to get a good intern position. But like I said, don't just focus on selling yourself. Let them go into sales mode as well – and aim to have them make you an offer. That's the whole bidirectional sales dynamic.

Also, after an interview I recommend that you send your interviewer a hand-written note of thanks. Emails are a dime a dozen. I don't know anyone who wants to receive yet another one, do you? And texting is too informal. Text your friends and family but please, not prospective employers. In contrast, hand-written thank-you notes are few and far between – and much appreciated. They distinguish you from the rest of the crowd. They signal that you really care because you took the five minutes to reflect. So write something on a card, put it in an envelope, find a stamp, and mail it. Once received, that card is physically permanent, and these days, a rare phenomenon.

To handle yourself, use your head.
To handle others, use your heart.

Eleanor Roosevelt

Authentic Presentations

In business we're always in the midst of a sales process in some form or another. Once you get your internship, or job after college, you'll regularly be presenting your work product – and every time you make a presentation, you're hoping to sell what you've done. You may be eager to receive recognition and perhaps even praise for your contributions. Your contributions are going to be evaluated partly by their initial look and feel. So of course you'll want to pretty it up a bit, format your work nicely so as to call attention to certain things.

Put yourself in your manager's shoes – what would you want to see and how would you want to see it?

When you honor your own work, the receiver will see this and honor you. You're not trying to put up a pretense in paying attention to looks – you're showing that you care about your presentation. And you're allowing the person receiving your work product to quickly assess its value.

Much will be happening simultaneously. You're in the process of selling yourself as a quality employee. If you feel humbly proud of your good work, you'll be seen as an authentic presence in the company. You're saying that yes, you want to put your best foot forward, while also being true to yourself. Your style and care in your presentation should be a reflection of your deeper nature.

Of course, there are many times at work when you're doing something new, something you might not quite know how to do yet – so be in open communication about learning something new. Don't pretend you know something you don't. Confidently explore what you're learning, and share how you are going about it. Leaping confidently into a new situation is the only way you're going to learn something new – learn by doing it. As you practice, you'll steadily develop and expand yourself. With enough practice, you'll get good at what you're learning to the point where it becomes an authentic expression of who you are.

It's wise to never be seen as embellishing or exaggerating your skills and abilities. Many people do that and sometimes seem to get ahead faster because they exaggerate their abilities. I personally find that it works better to be a bit understated, never acting like you can do something you're not yet ready for. If you don't overstep, if you prepare yourself adequately before leaping, you'll be praised for your courage and attitude.

In sum: if you authentically stay the course and develop your skills, then when opportunity comes to you, you'll be discovered. Hold to the virtues you most value, and trust in the power of goodness. An intern I worked with said this:

"I especially learned to value authenticity and kindness at work. It's so important to be completely honest with your associates and especially your mentor. I also very much value giving and receiving acts of kindness – we should care about each other's journey and be there for everyone we work with."

This approach to success also requires patience. That's why patience is a virtue the world over. It will keep you from getting over your skis, falling on your face and letting someone down. Instead you'll be able to adeptly accomplish what you say you can. Each time you do that, your confidence will grow, your personal power will expand – and you'll be able to enjoy your career's evolution each step of the way.

Overprepare.
Then go with the flow.

Regina Brett

What Work Suits You Best

Underlying the whole intern-search issue, in my opinion, is the deepest question – and it's two-pronged. What would you like to get really good at and what do you really enjoy doing? Said another way: what do you naturally enjoy focusing on in life and where do you want to apply your primary talents and abilities? If you can reflect on and answer these key questions, and then seek to find solid congruence where you have both of those in one profession, then you've set yourself up for both success and fulfillment over time.

I strongly recommend that you spend time on this twin question. If you don't get clear on these core issues, you'll end up wasting a lot of time – and in the end you'll probably not be satisfied with where you end up. So, how best to approach this challenge? We've already talked a bit about the art of practicing self-observation, where you pay conscious attention to how you respond to various situations in the present moment. Let's go a bit deeper into this primary mental function and apply it to this particular intent.

There are literally millions of companies in America involved in thousands of different types of activities. At first glance you may not realize which business themes, professions and practices carry special meaning for you. But once you start identifying what really lights you up and what you're especially good at, you'll begin to discover hidden realms in the business world that strongly attract you.

Do remember that internships, apprenticeships and mentor situations aren't limited to formal corporate positions. If you set yourself free in your self-discovery process, you'll find that whatever your passion and your talents might be, there'll probably be a way to make a living in that arena. It'll just take some creative thinking and maneuvering to carve out your own niche in the world's workplaces.

Furthermore, you'll find that as you fine-tune your passions and inclinations toward the type of work you truly want to do in life, you'll encounter mentors who are also interested in your passions – and they'll often be eager to guide you into realms of work you never even imagined existed before you started looking. But keep in mind that the first step, the driving impetus in this search, will always rest on your own shoulders.

You must take charge of initiating and carrying through to the end with your unique hunt for satisfying, meaningful and rewarding work. You've got to be responsible for your own development. Let's dig in deeper at the primary self-reflection level. You're probably not going to answer the passion/talent question immediately, so perhaps you'll want to schedule time to return to this section often in the next few weeks. I assure you that at some point you'll begin to feel genuine clarity emerging at both logical, emotional and gut levels of surety. Then you'll be ready to act with confidence in the directions that attract you the most.

Here's a basic process to move through at least several times if not more, in order to advance solidly on this inner path to clarity. You might want to have a pen and paper, computer or tablet handy, to write down what you discover:

First of all, take some time to look back into your early childhood for new clues about what you love doing. Get comfortable for a few minutes, let your mind quiet down as your breathing deepens ... tune in to all the various bodily sensations in this present moment ... temporarily let go of the future ... and notice how your breaths come and go all on their own when you stop controlling your inhales and exhales ...

And now, perhaps with your eyes closed, let yourself begin to remember doing something as a little kid that you really loved doing ... just relax and without any effort, see what early memories pop into mind when you were quite young, and playing around doing something that consumed your attention, and pleased you greatly as you did it ... relive having fun playing ...

Now you can just relax, reflect on what you remembered – and perhaps take time to write down what you were remembering. See what comes to you when you write down and complete the following sentence – and also take note of anything else that rises up into your mind:

"I remember when I was very young, having great fun while I was .... "

Pause & Reflect

~~~~~~~~~~~~~~~~~~~~~~~~

Your Favorite Things

In the last few generations, children have had less and less opportunity to play freely without adult supervision. This almost-universal loss of unstructured play-time is the unfortunate outcome of factors such as global modernization, parental need-achievement pressures, media-provoked anxieties and so forth.

Meanwhile, these days the young are being bombarded with so much buzzing media stimulation that their brains are developing literally quite differently than in earlier times. You yourself have grown a very different brain neurologically than your parents and grandparents. But still, as a human being, you pack the basic need to make sense out of your environment, develop heart-centered responses that enable you to bond with others, and find a satisfying life path where your primary passions are adequately expressed and received.

As you reflect on what you really enjoyed doing as a child, you'll find that your core personality was formed around what excited and held your attention. Even before you started school, and all the way through graduation from high school, there were certain people, events and things that strongly impacted or attracted you. By reflecting deeper into these experiences, you'll find new insights arising regarding what you might want to do when you get out of college.

Naturally your interests have matured since then, I'm not suggesting that you're going to return to adolescent games, pastimes, fantasies and activities. What's key here is tapping back into the feeling of being really passionate about something. Then you can easily connect that early free-flowing passion with related-but-more-mature expressions of your childhood interests. Through consciously establishing this emotional link with what excited you in younger years, you can approach your new passions with the same eagerness that motivated you back then.

As I suggested before, do make the effort to get your laptop or phone ready, or if you are old school grab a pen and paper – and after doing your memory exercise, take some notes on whatever memories, ideas and insights might come to mind:

> *Without any forethought or effort, after reading this paragraph you can close your eyes if you want. See what comes spontaneously to mind when you begin to look back and remember some of your favorite things to do at home or in school and after school. Don't judge what comes to mind, just fully relive experiences of doing what you really loved back then ...*

Look Back & Remember ...

~~~~~~~~~~~~~~~~~~~~~~~~~

Recalling Your Childhood Heroes

Now let's consider the people you most loved relating with when you were back in school before college. Along with what turned you off, who inspired you? Who awakened new horizons and ideas in your mind, and encouraged new adventures and discoveries as you began exploring the world around you?

What particular formal or informal groups did you like to hang out around and do things with? Who were your heroes as you grew up, both in real life and also in your imagination or in books, movies and so forth – who did you want to be like when you grew up? Your imagination has matured since then, so just let yourself enjoy remembering, without any judgment, who you admired and wanted to emulate in your own life.

> *Take some time to see who comes to mind. It doesn't matter if you now think your childhood heroes were fantastical or unrealistic. What matters most is remembering what they represented to you, how you felt back then about who you wanted to be like as an adult. Enjoy this trip down memory lane – and when you're done, write down what you remembered in as much detail as you can.*

*The only real voyage consists
not in seeking new landscapes
but in having new eyes.*

Marcel Proust

Valuing Passion

It's obvious that in all likelihood, working in a real-live company isn't going to leave you feeling like a hero in your wild childhood imaginations or in a movie. But this doesn't mean you have to give up your youthful passion for life in order to make a living. After all, a company whose employees have zero passion is a relatively-dead company. They do exist out there, in fact there are plenty of them – but you don't have to ever work for them. You always have a choice.

As you begin looking for an internship, you're going to run into all kinds of companies, from the livelier ones to the mostly-dead ones – and hopefully one of your priorities will be to join forces with a company where your passion for life can be openly expressed rather than hidden and diminished. You'll know fairly soon in your interviews which companies make you feel excited and eager and challenged, versus those that leave you feeling dead in your heart.

A root force underlying self-confidence is your determination not to ever give up your passion for achieving your optimum career. Companies that are upsurging into ever-higher success are in fact looking for new employees who will add passion and zest into the company equation. That's why I'm encouraging you to tap into and hold tight to that unique authentic passion that defines you, that has been driving your youth. Companies run on human energy. If you naturally radiate that sense of inner fire, combined with talent and training and cooperation – that's what will get you your dream job.

When you tie this element of passion into the process of successful networking we've been discussing, you'll discover a remarkably powerful formula for success. As an example, I'm passionate about sales. I always have been. So I have a lot to share with an intern related to my focus on passion in sales. When I find someone who shares my passion – that's a win-win. I'm naturally going to want to assist that person because it's satisfying to me to mentor people who resonate with similar interests.

As you re-ignite your deep youthful passions, you'll find that you naturally begin to come into contact with similar passions. You might discover them through the media or read about them, and as you study them you'll find out what makes them successful. And of course when you can, leap in and set up an opportunity to speak with these people. They'll probably want to talk with you because it's satisfying to share one's passions with like-minded people.

Especially begin to find people on campus who are a year or two ahead of you, students who've had experiences you haven't. Learn from them and their adventures. Ask them about intern situations they've had and envision yourself in their shoes. There's no substitute for talking to folks who have already done things that you perhaps also want to do.

This approach to getting a great intern job won't let you down. Just the opposite – one thing will lead to another. And I'm here to say that you don't have to stress out to get your preferred intern position. All you need to do is follow your passion, as they say – and marvel as your optimum job step by step emerges before you. This flow happens because you're in the zone, you're out there attracting what you desire through trusting and expressing your unique passion.

Here's another thing that's important. I've observed that the most successful people aren't always single-minded. Instead they often take two different things – two different passions, interests or talents – and get really good at both. Then they weave them together into an integrated value proposition. Consider carefully your primary talents and passions, and over time decide which two you really want to focus on in life – then weave them into your new expanded sense of purpose.

For instance, Yo-Yo Ma is one of the greatest cellists in the world. But that's not all he is. He's famous and successful because he wove his musical talent and passion for the cello into his parallel passion and talent for marketing cello music – his cello music! He combined his marketing skills and his masterful playing of the cello so successfully that now, if you think cello you think of his name. He may not actually be the best cellist in the world, but he certainly is the best weaver of cello playing and marketing.

As you take time to research successful people who share your passions and talents, observe how they've woven two elements of success into a winning strategy. Then see if you can internalize their attitudes and approaches to success. Imagine being in their shoes feeling their passion and their prowess. Generate a mental and emotional model clarifying this approach to fulfilling success in the world. Most importantly, when you interview for an internship be sure you stay grounded in this deep sense of who you truly are. This will enable your light to shine brightly and naturally empower you to advance toward the position you most desire.

Begin by always expecting
good things to happen.

Tom Hopkins

Do What You Want To Be

One of the things I say to people a lot is that leaders lead, traders trade, salespeople sell, and researchers research. If you want to be one of those, or anything else, then you need to start doing it now. Yes, right now. Do what you want to become. I don't care how this expresses itself in your particular situation. Perhaps you volunteer for a non-profit and learn to lead. Perhaps you sell surf boards. Perhaps you open an account with $100 and start trading stocks. Maybe you start researching an area of interest, like high-growth companies. It doesn't matter if you start with a very simple task anyone could do – what matters is that you start. And start now, not later.

As you do this, keep in mind that at your age you are continually changing. What you like this year may not be what you like next year. You're constantly evolving – but underneath your evolution there is a long-term process that's natural to you. It's carrying you through your entire life, based on your commitments and the resulting actions that you make, one after the other. That's who you are, and optimally you want to live continually within that process.

Another point. Many people, including me when I was in college, get impatient with where they are on their life-progression arc. During college this impatience is to be expected because you're still tied to school, not out doing your thing in the world. I remember distinctly during my sophomore year thinking, "Oh, my God, I've got three more years of sitting around studying, doing labs and going to lectures. I want to move faster and get out there." The clock in the common room would go tick, tick, tick, tick – and meanwhile my academic experience at Princeton was getting harder and frankly more miserable. I felt like I'd made a wrong turn off my life freeway and the next exit was a hundred miles down the road. I felt like I wasn't going anywhere at all. Nothing could be as bad as three more years of electrical engineering at Princeton.

So what to do when you feel that way? For me, I could have changed my major once I got clear about what interested me most in life. And also, once I knew the direction I wanted to aim in my life, I could have found an intern position that got me temporarily out of the academic world. By interning I could have moved into a more meaningful live-action experience in an interesting company. But instead, not seeing any alternatives, I foolishly decided to stick it out – and missed out on a whole world of other possibilities.

Of equal importance, I feel it's vital to also learn to relax in college and fully enjoy the present-moment experience – because that whole 'college interim' phase of life will soon disappear and be gone forever. Do yourself a favor, be nice to yourself, regularly let go of the looming future altogether. Laugh and enjoy your friends and all the fun of college while you're still there.

I now can see that I should have been an economics major or a philosophy major. With my EE degree, when I graduated I felt like I was finally free to step out and be me – but was that the real me? If I'd majored in something that truly excited me, I would have flowed into the next phase of my life much more easily. I would have connected with fellow students who loved what I loved, and I also would have bonded with teaching assistants and professors in an exciting field, and kept those relationships going to advance my career. But that wasn't how it went for me back then. Hopefully if you're in a rut in college like I was, this book will help you recognize that you are not alone, that you can gain clarity about what direction you want to go in your life – and then you can act on that clarity with confidence.

None of us can see the future, it's always uncertain. However, what we can do is intently look at our present situation, tune in to what really moves us – and then boldly take the next logical step in that desired direction. After you make that step, look around to see what the next logical step is – and take that step! After a few more successful steps you'll start to feel like, yeah, this is my path. There will always be unexpected twists and turns and difficult choices at the crossroads. You'll be continually altering your trajectory based on new information and opportunities and so forth. In the process you'll develop acceptance and confidence in your ability to make your own choices.

I also want to expand the whole notion of internships beyond just corporations and business settings. Sometimes your first step in a new exciting direction will seem to be a very curious step. Maybe you go off and apprentice in a traditional artisan trade like goldsmithing, or you spend what others might consider a wasted summer trekking through a part of the world to explore a culture that attracts you – and surprisingly your whole career expands into engagement within that region. Maybe you just go off to a monastery and sit quietly meditating on your breaths coming and going … and that leads you into a career researching the human brain's ability to enter into altered states.

It is all wide open. Anything is possible. Who knows where a seemingly-foolish step might lead you. If it's passionate and inspired and makes you feel like you're moving in the right direction – then do it! View the intern opportunity as broadly as you can. Get out there where you passionately want to be, and trust your own inner guide to move you heartfully into your optimum personal and professional niche.

College life is actually quite limited in scope. As we've been seeing, an internship is a chance for you to let fresh air blow into your life. An intern once told me this:

"While many college students might thrive in a classroom, an internship will expose them to quite new situations and unexpected problems. Being ready to fail at first in solving these problems, and seeing how more experienced people approach newness in general, will provide high value from an internship."

To end this chapter, perhaps you might want to take a breather and reflect a bit on what we've been talking about here. Here are some questions to ponder. Just let your attention kick into neutral for a few breaths … enjoy a bit of inner quiet after so much reading … and then see what thoughts, memories, imaginations and desires rise up as you read each question and breathe into whatever insights come to mind:

Right now, how do you feel about your major, your academic experience, and your situation in college?

Imagine ahead three years after graduation to where you're aiming to be in your career – how do you feel deep-down about your life goals? Is this really you, or are you still acting out your parents' or friends' vision of your future?

If money were not a concern and you could do anything for the summer, what would you really like to immerse yourself in?

If you could make just one step ahead of you, and that step could possibly determine your whole life trajectory, what step would you want to make?

How well would you say you really know yourself? What might be your deeper purpose in life?

And now, answer the following question by completing the sentence. Do this several times, until you really feel it's right:

"At least right now, what I really want to be in life is ...."

Chapter Six

EMBRACING IT ALL

~~~~~~~~~~~~~~~~~~

*We must have perseverance
and confidence in ourselves.
We must believe that we are
gifted for something.*

Marie Curie

Each time I bring a new team of interns into my consulting company, I prepare for them by remembering my own experience in college, which happened to be at Princeton University but in many ways could have been at most universities in America. I especially recall how I often felt lonely, frustrated and confused – which was probably fairly similar to many of my fellow classmates.

Everyone goes through a challenging shift when they leave home and find themselves out on their own, competing against thousands of other students who're playing the same highly-competitive and inherently stressful academic games. And on top of the academic stress, most college students don't really know where they'll end up after they leave college and plunge into the real world of earning a living.

It's quite natural, almost to be expected, that college students often struggle with self-doubt – the uncertain gut feeling of being adrift in a new world. I remember being internally weighed down with a whole bucket of issues ranging from anxiety about not succeeding academically, to guilt about perhaps letting down my parents, to feeling depressed about the lack of romance in my life. I remember trying to hide all these negative feelings, but inside they were almost constantly present.

Also – my career goals seemed to be withering away into an amorphous unattainable dream. My parents, as I mentioned before, were Palestinian refugees who'd emigrated to the U.S. after their marriage in the early 1960s. And while I was in high school, directly, indirectly or culturally, I came to understand an unspoken expectation of my parents that in college I would choose between three accepted professions: engineering, medicine or law. A major reason for my depressed confusion was that I felt little interest in any of them.

Watching my dad be a doctor over the years had taught me that even though he loved his work, I didn't really like the lifestyle that came with it. And law was out of the question because my reading speed wasn't exactly lightning, and sitting all day memorizing abstract legal concepts didn't speak to me. So having done well in math and science during high school, I'd signed up for courses that would prepare me for an engineering major – but the truth was that I felt almost zero passion for that career either.

I'd somehow assumed in high school that Princeton would be a bright supportive paradise where everything would unfold naturally to my benefit and pleasure – but I found my situation in many ways to be just the opposite. Thus my weekly trips to the mental health counselor. I wish every college student could have that luxury of personal help in resolving emotional issues. During these informal one-on-one sessions I learned invaluable new insights about what was provoking my bouts of guilt, embarrassment, anxiety and hopelessness.

Most importantly I remember learning to accept myself more and more just as I was – to stop fighting reality and instead to embrace every experience that came to me rather than feeling overwhelmed. I also learned how to get more actively engaged with my fellow students. Step by step, week by week, I found myself gaining a humble but expanding sense of who I was and what I might become in life. I often felt I learned more during just one of those hour-long sessions than in all my other courses combined.

These days as an intern mentor, I keep a constant eye on the whole notion of emotional support. I do my absolute best to offer my interns an environment where they can feel a sense of freedom and abundance. As their short-term guide, I strive to provide them with work experience they can build on for their careers – and also with the type of emotional support that lets them feel secure enough to explore who they really are at deeper levels.

I very much hope that more and more corporate intern-managers will also take on this 'trusted mentor' role so that this level of guidance becomes the norm. This comment from Lauren who interned with my company expresses the general spirit I'm talking about:

"I came into the work situation feeling very nervous and unsure of how to interact with Rob. He immediately put me at ease by developing a clear and open communication stream. He was very patient with my questions and qualms and trusted me to perform work independently. My confidence grew exponentially throughout my time at Agile."

I admit that I'm still learning how to mentor most effectively, and even most corporations are still learning how to approach internships. My intent here is definitely not to pick apart existing corporate programs. Instead, I want to spotlight new ways in which an intern and a corporate mentor can learn to work together toward the higher good. This rapid evolution of the entire intern process seems both natural and required, considering how our work culture as a whole is advancing these days. Ideally an internship will provide students with unexpected new heartfelt experiences of business life as their life-long career adventure begins.

The path to happiness
is found in accepting the moment,
not being controlled by desires and fears,
doing one's part in nature's plan,
and treating others fairly and justly.

Anonymous

Getting Real

In my experience, many college students are successful in putting on an exterior façade that all's okay in their lives, even if they're secretly floundering inside. We all have our superficial smiles and shallow social games that we can muster when needed, in order to present a positive and confident self-image. But ultimately, faking our way through life emotionally isn't a game-winner.

The hope of this book is that, when all goes well in your internship assignment, you'll have experiences that help you gain more genuine confidence about your coming career. You'll begin to sense that the business world out there can be friendly, supportive, creative and yeah, even downright fun. Rather than remaining submerged in academic learning and nonstop quizzes, papers and exams, you'll get a feel for 'real life' beyond college. You'll discover that in truth, you're limited only by your own limiting attitudes.

In my own college experience, by the time I graduated I'd somehow stuck with it and earned an EE degree. But I also broke with my parents' career expectations and lined up a beginning job in New York working not as an engineer but as a management consultant. By my senior year I was externally looking pretty good – I'd become a leader in my Eating Club and a wrestler on the varsity team. But deep down I wasn't feeling satisfied at all. I'd made many friends but I still didn't feel really connected to others or to what I wanted to pursue career-wise.

It's hard to explain but it seemed that the whole crowd around me was moving in a different direction than where I really wanted to go in life. I graduated in the class of 1990 and if I'd stayed in the field of electrical engineering like my parents initially wanted me to, the vast emerging universe of computer technology awaited me as a career. But with zero passion for semiconductors and computer design, I decided to just take a leap into the great unknown of consulting, even though I'd had very little training in that direction.

Heading off seemingly all alone right after graduation felt tough, to say the least. This is why I now do my best to design internships that allow students to explore and discover for themselves where their interests may lie. What I most needed while in college was something or someone to somehow pull me out of the whole ingrained mindset I'd grown up with, and still felt mostly stuck in. Deep-down I was hungering for some life-influence that would move me toward the new, toward a more optimistic vision of my future.

Said simply, I was starving for a mature friendly push in a fresh direction. So that's what I aim to provide the students whom I now mentor. I want to help them see beyond the gates of academia and all the preconceived notions of what business can and can't be. I want them to discover through hands-on experience that they are more than they think they are – and that the business world can offer far more than they might expect. I want my interns to learn how to feel real in that real world.

In this regard, during an intern program in my company, students will discover that there's no set agenda or curriculum.

With me, they're free to take the initiative of exploring pretty much anything they want to. The available client projects are adequately varied so that an intern never gets bored. Also, they usually work as a team so that they can learn from each other rather than compete with one another. I focus on assisting them in shifting up and out into a new perspective that's broader and more exciting than they expected. By the end of the internship I aim to have helped them realize that being their true authentic selves is the best path to success. And of course I do my best to lead by example.

The bottom line is that only by getting real do we become empowered. When we just do what others expect us to do, without thinking for ourselves about what we want, we generate very little manifestation power. But during our college years we can purposefully transition beyond being what our parents want us to be, if we choose to. We can experiment with dropping our fake façades. We can get real and insist on walking our own path through life, even if that path doesn't coincide fully with what our parents want for us.

At the beginning of the internship, I often get questions from interns like: "Am I just going to be working on one project alone the whole time?" I respond that no, they're going to have perhaps five projects – and that they'll be working on a team with several other interns rather than working alone. I also explain that because this is an entrepreneur intern program, we often don't know until about a month before the internship starts what projects we're going to be working on.

I assure them of just one thing – that I'll set them up to feel what it's like to experience winning in the business world. And

I deliver that. As their mentor I make sure that the downsides are low and the upsides unlimited. That's called positive skewness in finance and I apply it to life as well. That's the whole idea – to provide experiences that boost self-esteem and a positive attitude toward work in general.

Self-esteem is essential, but too often the college experience generates just the opposite. Students usually arrive at college with high self-esteem because they've performed well in high school. But college is so competitive that students often have their self-esteem knocked out of them, as happened to me. So it's vital to help interns start feeling that they're strong and resilient and able to succeed both in the perceived rat-race of higher education and also in their career expectations.

Part of my philosophy is to treat interning students so well and fairly that their self-esteem naturally strengthens. I know that this is the opposite approach of many intern programs that aim to 'keep the interns in their place' rather than lift them up. But in my opinion, the new generation needs support and encouragement and respect – they don't need to be treated like underlings living in the corporate basement. After all, they are the future!

Another thing that's important to me is paying interns fairly for their time and contributions. I pay enough for them to sustain themselves while working with me. But I don't promise them anything in terms of full-time employment in the future. Instead I make the present work experience invaluable for them – and then leave their future to naturally take shape.

Perhaps most importantly, I offer interns a sincere and caring relationship with a business executive. As a happily married father of two and a successful entrepreneur, I show them that everyone around me is being treated well and respectfully. My interns see clearly that this win-win approach to business and life does work – that even the interns entering my corporate sphere are fully appreciated and cared for. I design ways to make sure that my interns, as well as my clients, my company and my family, are provided the capacity and opportunity to be authentic and win in business and in life.

Toward this higher goal I offer my interns simple rules to explore such as: "When you're interning with me, you start at 9:00 am and finish work at 5:00 pm – and you don't work before or after that." Many companies work their interns way too long and hard. Some managers seem to be actually proud of how hard they drive their interns without paying them any overtime. Even now, knowingly or not, too many business leaders teach this next generation that work is mostly unfun, that you have to give up having a life in order to have a career, that dignity isn't part of the work equation – and that respect is only for those higher up.

Instead I tell my interns that they need to balance work and pleasure, on-time and off-time. Sure, if they have a passion for something related to their work, they can spend their off hours and weekends doing whatever they enjoy. Who am I to tell them that, for instance, downloading and analyzing cryptocurrency trades on Etherscan isn't a valid passion to indulge in, or that studying the history of energy regulation in Nigeria isn't a valuable and fun way to spend your weekend?

But I insist that they seek a balance, that they put in their hours with my firm and also take time to pursue whatever honestly thrills them. After all, exploring their driving passion is the only way to discover their true career focus.

As I hope all intern managers do, while I'm teaching my interns to ask for help when needed and to work confidently with a healthy work/life balance, I'm also teaching them to think forward and be well-prepared. I strive to be their partner as I listen for and support their greatness. This is my primary mentor role.

The only way to do great work
is to love what you do.

Steve Jobs

Transcending Apprehensions

Each and every intern is going to be nervous as hell about the first meeting with a client. I know that. What amazes me every time is how well they hide it and then acknowledge it later. After the meeting, they usually say, "Oh, that went so much better than I thought it would."

This initial nervousness happens even after I've given them significant training and guidelines. We've talked about each client and I've set it up for them to do really well on that first call. I've assured them that they're on a warm and welcoming team – but they're still nervous and hesitant about that first encounter. It's kind of like that very first dive off the high diving board.

And this brings up another thing – even if they're at a university like Princeton, which should give them a lot of courage and self-esteem, they're too often afraid to take a risk. There's so much fear of making a mistake. College should be a time in one's life to try new stuff, and yes, to fail sometimes. That's what learning is all about – taking risks and seeing what happens. But so many students are deathly afraid of being caught failing. They get embarrassed at even considering taking a risk and being seen in any way as a failure. The pain of failing is just too great, or so they think.

So they get to an internship and freeze up at the very idea of being on a video conference or visiting a client – simply because it's a new thing to do. The same dynamic applies to even asking a question. They don't want to be seen as stupid so they stay silent. But how exactly will they learn if they don't take risks and speak up? Unsurprisingly, I remember how I was the exact same way back then, and therefore missed opportunities left and right for growth and development.

Thus, I coach interns to break out of reflexive anxiety patterns that hold them back from experimenting and growing and winning. They urgently need to take leaps into the unknown, and to do this often enough so that they build up confidence that, even if they now and then 'fail' by asking a stupid question, the world doesn't end. Usually all the client wants is for the intern to do something accretive for them. The client isn't there to put the intern down. They are wanting them to succeed.

As I mentioned before, when I bring an intern into my advisory and consulting firm, often I don't know what assignments I'll be giving them until just a few weeks before. I might call a business associate I know and we'll brainstorm and come up with a mutually rewarding assignment for the interns. Perhaps at first it's a customer survey that's not overly challenging. I set things up for a win, and then the interns step in and do the work with the client.

Often the intern isn't quite sure what to do – but that's what being an entrepreneur is all about. You jump in and figure things out fast on the fly and then a month down the road some very good work has been accomplished and the client is pleased. And most important, the intern has risked and grown and learned and succeeded. They've had an experience of competence, fulfillment and joy. Even if the assignment was a mostly menial task that didn't take a lot of intellectual firepower, the uplifting taste of business success has been experienced.

> *The inferior person is worried and full of distress.*
> *The superior person is calm and at ease.*
>
> **Confucius**

Fairness and Sharing

Another important thing I do with my interns, which unfortunately is not what many other companies do, is that I don't pass off an intern's work as my own. The intern gets to experience working with a client, perhaps even with the Founder or CEO – and then at the end, the intern delivers that work and takes the responsibility and the glory of presenting their work. I provide guidance and feedback every step along the way, but the intern does the work – and learns in the process how to manage upward, how to talk confidently to clients and manage themselves.

A lot of times an intern will send me a draft of a report to look over before submission to the client. A common blind spot is that the report is too detailed or hard for an executive to read. I will aim to be supportive even if I have comments for changes – so that in the end it's still their report, but it is also what the client is looking for.

I'm fortunate enough to have been a chief operating officer of a $250-million hedge fund that I was the initial investor in. I have also been a leader in a very successful high-frequency proprietary trading firm, long before people knew what high-frequency trading was. At that company the growth was ridiculous – 25% per quarter for the three-and-a-half years I was there. I've been successful in my career through fostering relationships and developing unique skills that led into expansive business opportunities.

In response, I very much enjoy sharing what I've learned. Many business leaders seem to get their jollies out of not sharing. They prefer to always maintain a competitive advantage, relishing in information asymmetry. This stance is fine in trading, I understand that. If everyone knows what you know then your trading profits go to zero, or so the theory goes. But as a general rule I like to share, particularly with younger people. They're the future of our civilization. They're going to be running the planet someday. All of our lives will be affected by their decisions at some point. If we elders don't teach them well, we'll be provoking an unraveling of things. They need – and deserve – to benefit from the experience of previous generations.

How we treat the new generation is a direct expression of how others have treated us. I do my very best to treat my interns fairly, honestly and as equals, so that they can pass on this spirit of healthy business practice. I want to show them in action and not just in words, the foundation of a vibrant sustainable business environment. To do this, I don't focus over-tightly on what my interns accomplish. I focus on who they are, on who they're becoming, and on how they feel as they accomplish their goals.

Basically, I want them to feel, from the inside out, how to truly be a good-hearted win-win business person. Then they can evolve into someone who'll have a positive impact on the world around them. That's why I want to do what I can to lift them up and out of ingrained attitudes and limiting expectations. They need to discover a broader sense of who they are by shifting into a mindset that reaches beyond what they've inherited and brought to college.

I also want to encourage teachers and mentors to actively address the need of students to receive this deeper level of education. Parents too often assume that in college their children will magically come into contact with remarkable mentors who'll awaken them to a broader view of their future – but instead, the available mentors on campus may be few and far between, and meanwhile students get lost competing for top grades. They fixate on memorizing vast quantities of data for upcoming exams, and then quickly forget that data. In the process, they often lose touch with their deeper aspirations, with the joy of exploring new vistas in learning and self-discovery.

I regularly tell my interns that we should value life experience just as much as, or perhaps even more than, any particular accomplishment. By staying open to experiencing something new at their age, they can discover that their future is wide open – that they can develop new skills and perspectives, and advance into whatever work interests them the most. Anlin expressed this sentiment after completing her internship in my company:

"The internship was eye-opening for me in many different ways. We learned about different clients across several industries, and we had the chance to meaningfully engage in their work. Completing an internship is so fulfilling because you meet great co-workers and managers, you learn a lot about the industry that the firm is in, and you grow fast professionally."

I like to give my interns quotes from J.B. Fuqua, the Duke University Business School benefactor and namesake. For instance, here's one: "A temporary tolerance of mediocre performance leads to a permanent acceptance of poor performance." As you can see from all the many quotes in this book, the process of reflecting on potent sayings is important – because such quotes shine a light on and thereby focus attention directly toward core truths that, step by step, can take root within the mind, and even in the soul. After all, language is where being dwells.

*It is better to light a candle
than curse the darkness.*

Eleanor Roosevelt

Welcoming Mistakes

As I said before, interns too often try not to make any mistakes during a discussion. I've personally goofed many times in public and I still sometimes get caught feeling embarrassed by or even ashamed of my goofs. We're all human, we all make mistakes – and we need to constantly manage our self-judgment. Only when we're first kind to our own selves can we be productive positive members of society. When we make mistakes, we gain yet a new opportunity to be true to our whole selves, loving ourselves just as we are. Also, making mistakes and accepting them helps us to feel empathy for others when they make mistakes.

Once, I was asked to introduce the new dean of the business school at Duke University at a highly-regarded Chicago social club – and I did it really badly. Afterward I was utterly embarrassed and hated myself for not preparing more adequately. For years I anguished about it. But in reflection I was under a tremendous amount of stress right then. I was selling my business to my partner. He was quite young but already an extraordinary recruiter, which was the focus of our business. I did everything I could when I hired him to share ideas, contacts, information, everything. He sat in every meeting with every CEO we dealt with. I really was an open book, pouring everything into this young man – and we were making a lot of money. But after four years, when he wanted to buy the company and I wanted to sell it to him, the tone of our relationship soured completely and the tension around the transaction became near toxic.

The day when I was to deliver my introduction of the dean I was half out of my mind, not having slept well for weeks and stressed by not knowing what to do with my business partner. Will I sell the business to him or do we part ways forever? I was literally beside myself, seeing no way to move forward. And in that frazzled state of mind I got up to introduce the dean of a top-ten business school to fifty extraordinary business leaders in Chicago. I was in so much inner agony that a very simple thing like making an introduction tripped me up. I made a complete fool of myself, stumbling over my words trying to be funny but clearly being incompetent.

Shortly after that, my business partner and I confronted our situation – and something opened up between us and changed for the better. He took over the company and today he's a huge success. I couldn't be happier for him, we remain friends and talk to this day. But in the midst of selling the company I did totally mess up that introduction – and I had to realize that I'm human, that I make mistakes, that I can get in bad emotional states and do things I regret like freeze and not prepare.

No one is perfect, least of all me. I now channel that experience positively, and assure my interns that they have plenty of room to make mistakes. And when they do, they shouldn't beat themselves up about it – they should just pause, reflect, learn what they can, forgive themselves ... and move on.

The greatest enemy of a good plan
is the dream of a perfect plan.

Carl von Clausewitz

Valuing Newness

The bottom line is that I really enjoy working with my interns, they're high-quality students and we share a deep sense of mutual respect and admiration. I select them partly because they embody a quality of newness, freshness and openness to what's possible in their future. They come with what's called in the Zen tradition a beginner's mind – they acknowledge that they don't know everything, and they are humbly receptive to learning something new. They're willing to try and fail and then try again, all in the spirit of exploring the mysterious and discovering the new. If I allow those fresh young qualities to express themselves at work, it reinvigorates my whole company.

In contrast, I remember completing my MBA program at Duke and going to work in a bank's capital markets group in Chicago. I was on a team of recent MBAs from NYU, Indiana University, and the University of Chicago. We came to the company with the latest and freshest ideas from our universities – but our employer wasn't at all interested in what we had to offer. They just wanted us to plug in to how they went about their business.

I can't tell you how disheartening that was. I really learned something there – that if you're going to hire talented young people, you should openly embrace what they know, and tap into their budding vision of the future. Give them both permission and support so that they can genuinely move things forward for themselves and you.

> *Good, the more communicated,*
> *more abundant grows.*
>
> **John Milton**

Beyond Embarrassment

Often an intern's initial expectation is that I'll tell them what to do – they don't want to step forward and initiate anything. Perhaps they don't think they're even allowed to. In the beginning of the internship, whether summer or winter, there's often an underlying element of fear, apathy or lethargy. There's a reflexive hesitation to speak up and act, because they don't want to do something wrong and be judged and punished in some way. I've never met anyone who didn't have some of these 'hesitancy' issues – but to succeed at work, facing and transcending these concerns is crucial.

Shame, anxiety, guilt and embarrassment – these fear-based feelings that we heap upon our own heads are usually acquired before we even start school, and they definitely underlie the low self-esteem so many college students are hindered by. That's what happened to me when I flubbed my introduction to the dean and felt terrible for so long afterward. That experience generated trauma inside me not because of what happened, but because it pushed early-childhood anxiety-rejection buttons. Hopefully, interns can begin to decondition any such self-judgment reactions. Instead they need to strengthen their sense of self-worth – stop being afraid of doing something dumb or wrong.

When goofing up or doing something incorrectly, those reactive feelings of embarrassment and anxiety always come down to the ingrained fear of being kicked off of one's team, out of one's community – that core genetic fear of being exiled from the tribe. In the very old days, exiled human beings often died when they were kicked out of their clan. It's a primal fear of rejection that needs loving attention in order to transcend.

The solution is to learn to honor and love yourself just as you are – otherwise there's no chance of bouncing back. If you're always striving to be a perfect ideal version of yourself (which you'll never realistically attain) you're creating a no-win situation. That extreme mental programming needs to be evaluated – and then formally thrown out. It's a conditioned reaction that simply doesn't serve you. After all, the world didn't end when I flubbed my introduction to the Duke dean. I reacted as if it was a life-or-death disaster but of course it wasn't.

People are just as happy as they
make up their minds to be.

Abraham Lincoln

Giving And Taking Feedback

There's also a surprising amount of fear or judgment surrounding both the giving and the receiving of feedback. That's why I offer my interns a weekly one-on-one call. We talk face-to-face or through video call, practice sharing feedback, and learn to both give and take constructive criticism where needed, thus decreasing our fear of feedback. I also like to exchange feedback in writing as it offers a means to share that is less fear-laden, more natural and welcome in a relationship.

Although the main intern fear is usually fear of failure, many people also struggle with a fear of success. What if you actually get what you've wanted for so long? Everything might change in your life – and that can be anxiety-provoking too. You succeeded in getting into college, for instance, but that success may have led to new worries about letting your parents down if you don't excel in college. I recall worrying about letting down my friends and teachers from high school who truly believed in me. God forbid that after achieving so much in high school, I might fail at the next stage. What if I was just an impostor, not smart enough, not creative enough, not really as good as we all thought?

Fearing success can be wicked – who will I be if I succeed at high levels, will I even like myself or know myself if I'm rich? Will people not like me for just who I am if I have lots of success and power? If it's in fact lonely at the top, how will I deal with that? And what if I climb way high up – and then stumble and take a terrible fall? Gosh, what if I were worth a billion dollars? What if I write a book that's a best-seller – do I really want to totally change my lifestyle, be a celebrity and get locked in by my own success?

Sitting in college lectures and studying, students often don't run into these fears. But when you begin applying for internships you'll find that you begin to ask yourself – can I deal with failing if I don't succeed at my internship? And conversely, am I afraid of who I'll become if I succeed in attaining my dreams? These are important questions to reflect upon during the internship period of your life, so that you can prepare yourself for when you graduate and take on your first job.

The challenge of receiving feedback in your internship reflects all of these issues. Can you actually take criticism without reacting or freaking out? I admit that there was a time when I couldn't. One of my interns named Caroline said this to me:

"I would give all interns the advice to constantly strive to be open to criticism and even to ask for constructive criticism at the end of an interview or meeting. Admit that you're not perfect – that's the way to grow and advance."

Can you accept that you're imperfect, and yet at the same time perfectly okay just as you are? Life's full of such paradoxes. You'll want to expand your self-concept step by step to include the reality of all your imperfections and also the truth that you're perfectly okay just as you are right now. Unconditional love for yourself can, and in fact must, coexist with constantly striving to be better. Much of life is founded on such paradoxes. The challenge is to fully embrace your whole self.

Even before you start an internship, I recommend that you reflect on and prepare yourself mentally to regularly receive constructive criticism, or even sometimes not-so-constructive criticism – and at the same time, hold firmly on to your self-esteem. In other words, love yourself just as you are – and simultaneously open up to learn how you can improve!

> *Nobody's perfect, so give yourself credit*
> *for everything you're doing right,*
> *and be kind to yourself when you struggle.*

Lori Deschene

Fairness

The world is not fair. It never has been and perhaps never will be. It would take everyone – and I mean, everyone – agreeing on what fairness is, and then be willing to live by that sense of fairness. I observe that we actually still live in a paradigm of 'might makes right'. Those with power exert that power over people without power. Period. Fairness be damned! As you apply for an internship, you might be lucky and get into a company where fairness is the norm. But you might end up spending the summer or longer in a corporation that in many ways seems unjust to you, that violates your deep-down sense of fairness. What to do?

As I mentioned earlier in another context, whatever you do, don't just 'drop and run' when you get caught in a bad situation in your workplace. Instead, if you accept the situation as a rapid-learning opportunity, you can gain greatly by observing how a company functions when fairness isn't adhered to, when the virtues that supposedly hold humanity together are being violated regularly.

What in fact happens to human relating, to sharing, to communication – and to success? If you see this clearly in a negative expression with all its accompanying disastrous impacts, you'll later be able to set up situations in your career that avoid that unfair path and do quite the opposite.

Another thing I've learned is that, in every business situation, there's a lot more that we don't know than we do know. We pretend that we comprehend how the world works, even how the universe works – but as any honest scientist will admit, mystery is actually the norm. We can make fairly accurate predictions in certain realms of reality, but there are always hidden factors that can upset our plans.

That's why I encourage my interns to let go of trying to control everything around them. Instead, learn to flow gracefully with what's happening – make changes in flight regularly, based on unexpected alterations in the situation. Flexibility and acceptance are two important virtues to nurture, rather than rigidity and resistance. These are qualities that potential employers will be looking for keenly.

Flexibility and acceptance will allow you the space to admit that you don't know everything and be ready and willing to change your attitude and beliefs when new information comes flowing in. No one likes a know-it-all. Why? Because people who act like they fully understand every situation are not being honest, they're being arrogant – and they'll be the last to admit to mistakes and take actions that will improve a situation.

When you arrive for your internship, the attitudes you bring with you will definitely influence your ensuing experience – so it's wise to keep an eye on your reactions, your assumptions, your willingness or unwillingness to let go of attitudes that don't ring true for the work you're doing. For instance, if you're carrying the attitude that you won't work for anyone who's not being entirely fair, you'll need to reevaluate in order to participate in the situation.

If you're in a situation that doesn't seem fair in some regard, naturally you'll want to see if you can improve that situation in the direction of fairness. But similar to accepting yourself just as you are, in order to change a bad or unfair situation you must first accept the situation just as it is. You must find out why things look the way they do. Maybe the situation is actually more than fair, given some additional history. First take time to see the situation clearly. Then discover how you might be able to improve it. Again it's a paradox, and an important one to understand.

It's unfortunate that we don't often teach these things in college. The collegiate atmosphere strives to be fair all the time – but 'real life' in the workplace includes all types of people, very good and very bad and everything in between. So be prepared in your intern position to deal with whatever comes your way. Acknowledge it, understand it, accept it, learn from it – and of course, change whatever you can for the better. Most importantly, ask yourself: "If I were running the show, how would I design this differently?"

> *Happiness is a function*
> *of accepting what is.*

Werner Erhard

Stay In Your Body

Our society sees intelligence primarily as a cognitive function of the mind. For instance, you were accepted into your university primarily on your intellectual talents and development. But as we mentioned before, your emotional intelligence is also important – perhaps even more important than your cognitive intelligence for living a fulfilled life.

Your emotional intelligence is based on your feelings, and your feelings are based on how well and deeply you experience your emotions as a whole-body happening. So when you head off to do an internship, do remember your whole-body presence will be as important as your intellectual acumen.

If you're absolutely brilliant mentally and yet a total drag to be around emotionally, chances are you're not going to succeed. Sure, some people who are emotionally difficult do rise to the top in business. But generally speaking, if you want to be a leader in business or even a successful mid-level player, your success will partly depend on whether people like being around you as a whole-body presence.

This might sound obvious, but I bring up the issue again because right when you arrive for your internship you're probably going to feel anxious – and what happens when you feel anxious? You tend to lose your awareness of your bodily presence. And what happens when you do this? The people around you pick up on and react to your anxious condition, especially if you compensate for your condition with non-authentic behavior.

It's important to anticipate this possible scenario and do something about it. For instance, you'll want to practice staying aware of your breathing and being present in your body before you enter your intern workplace so that you're good at being authentic when the time comes to shine. Remember that in school you've been constantly rewarded for being out of your body, lost in thought and calculation deep inside your mind. Now you need to prepare for the real world by exercising your awareness muscle that keeps you grounded in your physical presence – especially while talking with people at work.

The simple truth is that when you temporarily lose awareness of your own breathing and bodily presence, there's really 'no-one home' for others to relate with. Anxiety provokes this loss of presence – and anxiety is very much a physiological thing. The path to transcending anxious feelings is to stay aware of your body, your breathing, and your inner feelings. You do this by consciously focusing your attention exactly where anxiety makes you lose awareness.

The process for strengthening your physical and emotional presence is fairly simple, but it requires that you take this training seriously and devote time each day to becoming self-aware and self-confident. You'll do best to practice this process first alone, then you'll want to practice it when talking with others.

Here's the basic flow. Read through the process a couple of times to begin, so that you start to memorize the steps. At the end of the book we'll provide a link to an audio guidance so that you can relax your mind as you move through this 'here and now' experience often enough to make it a strong habit when you need it:

Just get comfortable where you won't be disturbed for five minutes or so. Settle down, and now tune in to your breathing. Make no effort to breathe, just honestly look to your breathing – and you'll discover your current emotional condition.

Focusing on your breathing will become your primary life-line reality orient for bodily awareness. You'll find that as you watch your breaths going effortlessly by, your emotional mood will begin to change for the better – with each new breath you'll calm down and let go of your tensions and worries, and regain some good feelings inside your body.

Notice that when you hold your full attention on the actual physical sensations you're feeling in your nose right now, your chronic flow of thoughts become less dominant, more and more quiet ... and then can temporarily fade entirely – this is what you want to have happen. This is what mindfulness meditation is all about, just breathing consciously and regaining your senses in the present moment.

Now you can expand your awareness to include the breathing movements in your chest and belly, as they expand and contract with each inhale and exhale. Accept whatever feelings you find inside you, and watch how they relax with each new effortless breath ...

And now, while you stay aware of your breathing experience, gently expand your awareness to also include the feelings in your feet ... and expand again to also include the feelings in your legs ... in your pelvis ... in your hands and arms and torso ...

And now expand your awareness again, to include your throat, your tongue and your lips ... stay with your breathing as you also include the muscles in your face ... around your eyes ... and the top of your head.

Now you can just relax entirely, and enjoy the primal feeling of being alive in your whole body, here in this present moment.

And right in the middle of this experience, go ahead and tune in to whatever feelings you find in your heart ... accept those feelings, breathe into them, and say to yourself, "I love and honor and accept myself and all my feelings."

Good! I strongly encourage you to practice this five-minute whole-body awareness process several times each day. Also practice this relaxed quality of awareness with other people, whether you are talking to someone or when you're quiet and listening in someone's presence. When you listen in this receptive state, people will feel thankful that they're really being heard.

Set your goal to do this anxiety-reduction whole-body meditation at least once a day for the duration, so that you're always ready to shift into this expansive high-presence awareness whenever you're with someone or getting ready for a meeting. And take this powerful emotional skill with you to your internship!

Chapter Seven

STANDING IN THEIR SHOES

~~~~~~~~~~~~~~~~~~~~

*A good leader inspires people
to have confidence in the leader.
A great leader inspires people
to have confidence in themselves.*

Eleanor Roosevelt

There needs to be a deep personal benefit on both sides of the intern/mentor equation for it to be successful. To maximize this benefit, you'll want to regularly ask yourself: "What is my mentor or manager getting out of this relationship?"

Holding that query in mind will be a great step into a new level of maturity for you. Just take a bit of time each day to pause, tune in to your breathing, and in the spirit of kindness, consider what the other person in a relationship is wanting, needing and receiving from their interactions with you.

There's of course a direct benefit to any company from having fresh relatively-inexpensive labor on the team. But beyond that, what's the benefit to that specific business person, the executive manager who's taken on the responsibility of an intern for a summer, winter or semester? What's the payoff internally for them in doing this? Why should they shift and learn how to run an internship program, especially one designed like we're describing in this book? What's motivating them and what will satisfy them?

I spent a whole month designing my first intern program before my initial interns showed up. And I admit I designed the program not only for the interns but also for myself. We too often think of a successful business person as hard-nosed, driven by numbers, hungry for profit and monetary success. But of course, people in business are still people – they have other needs besides business success. They have emotional needs, relationship needs, social and even spiritual needs. For me, the internship program is an opportunity to fulfill many of these needs along with the stated business intentions.

So, back to you, what do you think you might have to offer someone who is older and more mature and experienced than you? This is a key question to ponder before and while you're interning. And here are a few ideas that might resonate with you.

Perhaps your manager simply wants to enjoy a warm-hearted friendship with a college student, a sharing of good feelings – and perhaps a much-needed sense of lightness and new vision that you can bring into the company. Are you able, willing and eager to provide this type of optimistic, heartfelt input? Is your heart open to exploring a new and, of course, entirely-platonic friendship? As one intern put this:

"Fun in the workplace is possible even in desk work. Sharing good feelings is optimally how work should be."

Also, many experienced people actually love to teach others what they've learned in life. On your side, are you prepared to be a good learner, can you be quiet and listen to someone sharing their perspective, can you learn – and also express gratitude? A teacher loves to see students absorb and then run with a new idea or insight. Are you going to naturally fulfill your mentor's need to teach an intern – and will you be openly thankful for what's being offered?

Your success in pleasing and satisfying your intern manager will be very important on several fronts. First of all, if you get along as friends and colleagues, you'll both be uplifted at work. If there's a positive charge between the two of you, you'll find that your mentor focuses more attention in your direction and you benefit from the relationship at higher levels.

For instance you'll learn a lot about the psychology of business relationships. You'll learn through alert observation and interaction how to communicate with clients and fellow workers – and at deeper levels you'll discover the magic that happens when you're fully engaged on a harmonious team that gets things done.

Always keep in mind that your intern manager might be an important network link later on. This person can write recommendations for you, hold you in mind for future employment, and perhaps introduce you to opportunities you'd never otherwise find. You're being given the chance to learn not just a particular line of business but also the general skills of win-win empowerment and communication.

To succeed in this world
you have to be known to people.

Sonia Sotomayor

Becoming More Other-Centered

None of these positives in an intern relationship will happen if you're habitually stuck with your attention fixated on yourself. All of us are self-centered of course, because we're in charge of running our own ship – but being self-centered is very different from being self-absorbed. I keep harping on this basic theme because being a student for over a dozen youthful school years has unavoidably conditioned you to fixate on your own intellectual development as well as your advancement relative to others. But when you suddenly drop into an intern role off somewhere in a company, you'll need to rapidly shift into a new gear – a gear of working on a team where you're not the most important thing happening in the room.

As we've seen, one of the best ways to achieve this shift is to temporarily get out of your head and into your body and your feelings. If you're not fully present as an emotional entity when you relate with your manager, the whole thing is going to stagnate. School reinforced being busy performing acrobatics with your cognitive function. When interning you'll be expected to show up as a whole person, contributing not only busywork but also creative insights, enthusiasm, patience and, when needed, help in raising the mood of your team. This will require that you regularly dig down into your heart, into your feelings and be true to yourself as a whole person who's open and exploring what work has to offer.

Of course, you might end up with a manager who's also fixated on cognitive performance – and when this happens you can be the one who initiates an expansion of the relationship to include more heart-felt dimensions at work. For instance you might do this by asking how they feel about the work being done, or what their expectations may be about the future of the company.

As you do this you'll discover that in fact, you can have quite an impact on a company by being emotionally bright and present rather than dull and absent. And you'll find that the more you let your emotional resonance radiate with positive vibes, the more you'll find others wanting to work with you on the team.

There's a fine balance you'll need to evolve into – between being friendly as you take time to relate personally and being professional and holding your focus on the work at hand. Hopefully your mentor will teach you in action about how to maintain this balance. But if not, you'll need to explore it for yourself.

Again, what's key is striving to be as genuine, honest and authentic as you can – all the time! In this regard a good mentor will meet you where you are. They'll find out your motivating interests and where you see yourself heading in the future. They'll sometimes step in and assist you in taking the next step toward success in an assignment. Often your beginning assignments will be fairly mundane – but even in very simple assignments you'll discover opportunities to try out new ways of getting a job done, and also new ways of relating with people around you as you do things together.

You'll perhaps also be able to observe a top-notch executive at work – see how they relate, where they focus most of their attention, how they manage their time. Learning by osmosis is very important! There are many subtle nuances you can pick up on when observing the best in action. And don't be fooled by things that look easy to do. All levels of excellence are equally difficult, and it takes years of intellectual rigor and focus to make it seem simple.

And keep in mind that as you observe, you're also being observed. Don't be self-conscious, but do be self-aware. If you're given a simple assignment, for instance, and you do it fast and well, then you'll be in a better position to be given more responsibility.

Also, don't forget that your job is first of all to make sure your manager looks good. You'll need to manage your inner feelings so that you stay mostly positive, friendly and receptive, no matter what might be happening. This bright confident stance will enable progress to occur as efficiently as possible. From such a positive emotional foundation you'll begin to build your professional skills and goals with your manager as your ally.

We can choose to take responsibility
for our moods.

Fernando Flores

You As Witness

There's a quality of consciousness known as 'being the witness' or 'the observer' or maintaining a 'neutral posture' – and developing this quality as an intern can be deeply rewarding. It involves being highly observant, but not reacting to what you're observing. No one wants an intern who's constantly over-reacting to what's happening and getting themselves in the way as a result. Instead, I recommend that you develop the high-order ability to see what others are doing without reacting.

The trick to this is simply to stay neutral, grounded in your own calm confident center as you witness what's taking place around you. Hold a calm emotional presence that will help others when they're caught up in their own reactions. By practicing this 'witness' role you'll stabilize the emotional atmosphere at work and you'll learn a great deal from quietly observing the dynamics of a difficult situation at work.

When you practice being more other-centered, life flows much more naturally. Being interested in others enables others to also be interested in you. When you're quiet and observant, people will in fact notice you more in a positive way than if you're constantly reacting. You're expressing natural poise and intelligence, radiating an aura of budding wisdom even at your young age. You'll meet people's eyes but not disturb their discussion. You'll feel quiet and yet stay engaged – and of course you'll speak up when you have something constructive to offer.

The word 'listen'
contains the same letters
as the word 'silent'.

Alfred Brendel

Turning It Off

Here's another dimension of an internship that I want to mention, even though I know that some intern managers will strongly disagree with me. The general theme here is often called the work/life balance. Most interns assume that they're going to be worked half to death during their internship and so they plunge into their assignments 24/7. Some can't wait to work those long hours as a badge of honor. They want to show their employer that they have the dogged discipline and blind passion to put aside all other aspects of their lives – that they can devote their full attention to work.

My advice is – let go of the assumption that you'll succeed at higher levels if you negate your personal life. In my opinion you'll end up doing just the opposite. Being all business and nothing but business is not a good way to live life. You're setting yourself up for physical, mental and emotional pain, and predictable burnout, plus you're making yourself unidimensional in the process.

To be sure, many businesses run at break-neck speed and demand that you sacrifice family, friends, avocations, fun and everything else in the name of work dedication. However, more and more companies are realizing that in the long run, employees who have a healthy family and social life are much more productive and creative than employees who are singularly focused on working themselves to the bone all the time. I knew a workaholic executive who, even though his work was extremely good, lived basically all alone with no real friends or nurturing pastimes to enjoy after work. It was a sad situation.

When interviewing for an internship, and later on when searching for full-time employment, make sure you look for a position where your whole being will be appreciated – where you're not only allowed to but expected to have a life outside of work. If you're actively hunting for a company that's bright emotionally and eager for your whole being to participate on their team, you'll surely find what you're looking for. In life, you do find what you are searching for. Wise companies right now are looking for people just like you.

I find that with my interns, I often need to actively push them in the direction of having a life. I appreciate interns and colleagues who genuinely love their work and put their whole souls into a project. That's wonderful! But I also very much value people who can readily turn it off – who can consciously say to themselves, "Okay, I've put in my hours, I've done a good job today and now I'm done. I'm going to walk away from work for the evening, or the weekend, and thoroughly enjoy myself."

I remember a situation where one of my interns needed a day off for travel. I thought, fine – and then I decided to have my other interns get a day off too. My one requirement was that they truly take the day off and practice relaxing and enjoying doing nothing – no work of any business kind! Some people find that challenge very difficult to do – turn it all off. They've been conditioned to push themselves constantly, as if they're never allowed a break in life.

Self-inflicted, nonstop treadmills are pernicious because if you can't turn it off, somewhere down the line you're going to end up running on empty and suffer from loads of problems. A lot of us work ourselves nonstop in order to avoid negative memories and emotions that otherwise rise to the surface – but it's vastly better to stop and resolve those feelings than to constantly run from them until they overwhelm you. Really.

My interns found this 'time out' assignment very difficult to accomplish, so we talked it all over later and shared our various ideas and experiences. They weren't sure why I'd given them that strange 'turn it off' assignment, so I said, "Look, I don't want you guys to graduate from college, get a job, maybe get married and have kids – but then get a divorce or be an absent parent because you never learned to turn it off. If you can't snap out of the work buzz when you walk out of the office, you're not going to have a good full life. Besides, what's the point of working so hard, pushing yourself financially and professionally, if your life at home is a pretense-laden quagmire?"

As an intern you'll be developing your long-term adult work habits. You'll be discovering how you personally prefer to balance the work and non-work phases of each day. Right from the start, be sure to pay attention not only to when you're at work and off-work, but especially to the transition time between work and off-work.

Life is full of transitions, where you shift from one situation to another – and negotiating these transitions is crucial to a good life. You need to rapidly ramp up when you go to work and you likewise need to drop down into your emotions and relative relaxation when you leave work. Your intern experience will be a great opportunity to see what an optimum business life can look like – where you value your personal life equally to your professional life.

I encourage you to pay close attention to who seems especially good at the work-home transition – and learn from them. Also observe who's not good at turning off the work buzz – and see how their lives unfold. Meanwhile for yourself, when the work day is done you can consciously practice whatever helps you to decompress and delve into open free time. Learn how to flip off your mind's work computer and set your fun-play spirit loose to run free for a few hours or a weekend.

Maybe you'll learn to practice mindfulness meditation to make this shift. Maybe it's sports that sets you free, maybe it's hanging out with friends, playing an instrument or just goofing off for a while. Perhaps you might encourage some romance to percolate into your life. Whatever you find that works, discipline yourself to be temporarily undisciplined! Turn your focus of attention in new directions, find a passion that ignites you off-hours – something that is hopefully also a healthy use of your time.

If you start 'turning it off' each evening early in your career, you'll establish holistic habits that will make your life vastly more fulfilling than if you let yourself become a die-hard workaholic with no fun or emotional growth in your life. You can also use the process you began to learn in the previous chapter as a core transition meditation away from cognitive buzz into whole-body emotional presence. In five minutes once you get good at it, you can confidently break from work each day and effortlessly set yourself free.

Three O'clock Burnout

In my observation, most people come into their workplace in the morning full of energy, ready to run with their assignments. But around three in the afternoon there comes a lag. Not much gets done after three in the office – or if it gets done it's not done especially well. I've noticed this with myself over the years, as well as with employees. So, with my interns, I usually teach them a different pattern than just pushing doggedly until it's five and time to quit.

I structure the work day for interns by beginning with a short meeting to let them get complete about the previous workday and last night or the weekend. They then talk over what they intend to accomplish that day. As J.B. Fuqua says, "When people establish their own objectives, they are more committed to the achievement of those objectives." Then at three we end that work push, and get together to talk over the day thus far. I then ask them what they might accomplish, on any front, from 3:30 until 5:00? Their basic day is done – and now there's an hour and a half to do something more, perhaps in a different mode or mood. We make that last 90 minutes a game: "What can you accomplish with fresh interest and energy until five?"

What I find is that, instead of those last two hours being wasted with minimal accomplishment, after half an hour of reflection, review and planning, their minds are again energy-charged and ready to dive into something new and interesting.

In 90 minutes, what can you accomplish? If you take a moment to ease up and reflect on your accomplishments thus far and then find something interesting to work on for 90 minutes, you'll often experience new energy flowing within you. A lot more can get done now in an enjoyable fashion.

When I initiate this experimental approach into the workday, I find that my interns begin to look at their whole schedule in a more inventive way. They begin to realize how they spend their daily energy. Do they waste it? Do they use it up too fast? What other alternatives can maximize productivity and work patterns? After all, we only have until 5 pm daily. That's it! So, I want my interns to realize that business patterns aren't set in stone. They're malleable. Business is constantly evolving, and they are too.

We either learn early to let ourselves evolve in our work environments – or we're liable to establish habits that lead to stagnating and falling behind the competition. An intern I worked with put it this way:

"In many ways I realized that I was practicing habits and developing attitudes that would follow me for the rest of my career. And so I started paying more attention to what habits I really wanted to live with into the future."

The 30-minute conversation at 3 pm, coupled with those last 90 minutes of a workday, can also be an opportunity when a manager and interns find time to get to know each other at deeper levels. Like I said before, wise managers are well aware that if the intern-manager relationship blossoms, the fresh perspective of an intern can revitalize a company – and interns can discover that they do have something to offer. But this happens only if they relax into their role on their work team, see the direct results of their actions, and consciously witness the functioning of the company.

Burnout is nature's way of telling you
that you've been going through the motions,
but your soul has departed.

Sam Keen

Chapter Eight

EMPOWERED TRANSPARENCY

~~~~~~~~~~~~~~~~~~~~~

Love what you do.
If you haven't found it yet, keep looking.
Don't settle. Stay hungry. Stay foolish.

Steve Jobs

As we've seen, a college internship is very often the starting point of a person's business career. An internship can be the ignition point where you begin building a lifetime of work that's enlightening and valued as a service to humanity. Even if you end up in a mediocre, downright boring and frustrating intern assignment, you can learn plenty about what not to do in business. Like I said earlier, channel the frustration into something positive for your future.

To benefit fully from your internship, it's vital to keep a part of your awareness operating in detached-observer mode so that you can reflect upon and realize what's being learned in your internship. That's why I recommend setting aside a particular time in each day or evening to make entries in your journal. If you pay full attention to all your emerging experiences and insights, you'll gradually and authentically empower yourself to become a leader further down the ever-twisting road of success.

Especially make notes on your intern manager. I like to ask intern mentors this question: "What are we teaching the next generation about our corporate culture?" Culture – how things get done – matters. It's what an intern actually walks away with when the assignment ends. As intern mentors, how can we set a hopeful and even inspiring example of optimum business spirit and practice?

If we accomplish this mentor goal, we might spark a whole new era of possibilities in the workplace and help stimulate a positive evolution in the business world. In this sense, as the creative designers of internships we become responsible for shaping that future.

Nurturing An Experimental Spirit

In a healthy thriving workplace there is definitely a bright spirit of innovation and experimentation. One of our most powerful human abilities is our capacity to explore new ways of doing things. I always want my interns to feel free to try something unusual and divergent from the norm – to risk failure in order to perhaps find a better approach. I'm not an expert on education or psychology, but one thing I'm very good at is learning from my own mistakes – maybe because I've made so many.

I've learned that it's extremely important to navigate through our own unique experiences without negatively judging ourselves. We discover what's possible only through inspired experimentation – and over time, that's how we become powerful, valuable leaders. But to feel free to trust our personal insights and out-of-the-box possibilities, we first need to become really good friends with our inner selves. We need to value our own uniqueness and observe how we contribute to the uniqueness of the people around us.

We're living during a phase of history where everything is becoming mass-produced, digitized, full of data content but devoid of personal uniqueness. Impersonalization, especially the lack or the denial of human emotion and connection, is ripping our society apart. So many employees have minimal power to make individual choices and decisions. Their jobs are confined in a tight box. This seems to me very dangerous – and something we need to push back against.

When a work culture insists that its established rules be almost worshipped rather than experimented with, we take away a company employee's sense of value, initiative and self-respect. During the last 100 years, technology has seriously transformed how we see ourselves – it's even transformed the neural wiring of our brains. More and more, the intuitive wisdom and creativity of the human mind and heart has been minimized. Traditional qualities like integrity, authenticity and creativity have been pushed aside in the name of conformity and computer-driven management.

In essence, we've sidelined the vast creative power of the individual human and relegated employees to extremely low-responsibility positions in the workplace. Ingenuity and inventiveness are too often judged as negatives that threaten to disrupt the mechanical computer-driven uniformity of contemporary life. More and more jobs are about thinking less and less. This is a sad period for so many human beings at creative and emotional levels. By allowing ourselves to be dehumanized by heartless technologies, we are in fact ultimately endangering the very fabric of our society – making our work lives unenjoyable and unfulfilling.

I feel that the intern-mentor relationship offers us a very bright opportunity for returning the human-based qualities of uniqueness, empathy, creativity and joy to the workplace. If there's one primary realization I want students to get out of their internships, it's that people count. I want them to see that there is great value in always looking to see a real caring human being on the other side of each and every interaction.

Why? Because when we fully value the person we're doing business with, and when we see and accept and love them as the whole human being they are, then life comes flowing vibrantly back into the business equation. Valuing the whole person empowers them to experience themselves as creative, heartful, fair, honest and supportive.

In this broad context, collaboration and creativity are set free to blossom. And within this mutually-trusting atmosphere we can all enjoy the rush of occasionally experimenting and exploring new ways of doing things – and our business can then thrive.

To build a long-term, successful enterprise
when you don't close a sale
open a relationship.

Patricia Fripp

The Virtue Of Transparency

I'm a big fan of transparency in business. Even a tiny thing being hidden or held back in a communication can undermine the whole relationship. There's a solid reason why all cultures value honesty and integrity so highly – because when these qualities are missing, everything in life becomes more complicated, antagonistic, difficult and devious. When openness and trust are lost, suspicion rules and disaster looms nearer and nearer.

Put simply: when you're hiding anything at all from someone, your attitude of deception will have room to take over the atmosphere of the relationship. Choosing to deceive someone regarding even a very minor point is like letting just a slight contamination of a virus into your system – it's liable to take over and contaminate the whole situation. You end up losing your ability to be totally straight on any front with this person.

Likewise and even more damaging – when you're dishonest about some small point with just one person, you begin to see yourself as not entirely honest with the world. Your self-identity takes a massive blow – you no longer consider yourself an honest person. To compensate for that, you'll even begin to deceive yourself. In short, lack of transparency is not a wise path to follow in the long run.

Lack of transparency also indicates that you're afraid of revealing something. In fact, dishonesty always reflects an underlying anxiety about revealing the truth of the matter. To see that being dishonest is rooted in being afraid is an important step toward making transparency a primary virtue in your business life.

We are all human, so we will make the mistake of withholding information or saying something that is untrue, often unintentionally. When you do so, act right away to clean it up as soon as you notice it. This will engender trust. Perhaps seek advice on how to best express what you need to say or do in order to restore the relationship. I have found that increasing my vocabulary around certain issues assists me when I need to express something challenging.

The bottom line is: stop undermining your success by harboring any fear of openly revealing the truth of the matter. Even if it's a tiny untruth or hidden fact, you'll find it important to immediately correct it. Untruths will accumulate and limit what is possible in your life – so it seems wise to stop that process ... right now.

I'm sure you can guess by now that in my opinion, the relationship between intern and mentor needs to be grounded in full transparency – no hiding anything. No pretending to be what you aren't. No fear of revealing who you really are. No false expectations or secret judgments. Instead, use the intern-mentor relationship as an important new experiment in nurturing authenticity, openness and mutual trust.

In this spirit, there always comes a time during an internship in my company where I say, "Okay, today I'm going to open up all the company books so that you can experience total transparency in action." Then I log in and show them on the screen how much we make from this and that client, what our agreements look like, how much everyone gets paid, and what our expenses are in detail. I go through the last couple of months with them, showing what came in, what went out. The company bank account is on full display along with all the credit-card statements.

At first, some interns aren't sure what to think when openly shown all these usually-hidden dimensions of a company. But this is one of the major purposes of an internship – seeing under the hood, so to speak, and realizing that I'm not afraid for them to see everything about my company. I acknowledge that it requires a leap of faith each time for me to do this, because I know there might come judgments and opinions about some things found in the books. Agile Rainmakers is not perfect. But after I've been purposefully honest about everything, I find that I feel no fear at all of being exposed or found out. Instead, a very good feeling of profound trust and mutual respect arises – and this is such a marvelous feeling!

It's a very sad fact that so much of business in the world is based on not only trying to be secretive, but also lying and cheating whenever possible, in order to make a buck. For many thousands of years, people have tried to cheat on their taxes, for example – as if being an honest person is a dumb game to play, and integrity doesn't matter. From what I can tell, I am a rare transparent tax payer. I gladly pay my taxes because I know logically that if I don't pay my fair share – and everyone does the same – then who's going to pay for the police, the fire fighters, the roads, the snowplows, the streetlights, the military, and the care of the impoverished and elderly?

Not wanting to pay our fair share of taxes, and actively looking for ways to avoid doing so, is basically saying we're choosing to be freeloaders in life. Many wealthy folks are clever in their justifications, but at the end of the day they are simply unmitigated freeloaders. I prefer to keep it simple and do my part. Philosophies and religions I've studied teach us to do our share and not cut corners – so what are we doing when we teach our kids that being deceitful in business or with the government is an acceptable path to success? Being dishonest leads to further distance with others – it generates anxiety, slows things down, and ultimately results in failure.

I share my feelings on all of this with my interns, that's part of the mentor role in my opinion. But I don't dogmatically insist that my way is the right way. I just say that I've found that being honest and fully transparent works best for me. They can walk away and say, that's pure genius – or they can walk away and say, that guy's a moron. They need to be free to decide what works for them.

My job as mentor is to honestly share what I've learned from my experience, and then they can build on that in whatever way works for them. For example, I have a special client-advisor agreement that I consider to be partly responsible for my company's success – and I share this agreement openly with my interns. It begins with the standard two pages where

I *promise* to do this and that, for such-and-such payment schedule – all the usual details. But then comes a third page, a unique addendum designed to maximize the full opportunity of working with each other. The page also states that I *recommend* the client strive to do the same as I promised to do.

Basically this addendum clarifies what we've been talking about in this book – that both Consultant and Client agree to strive continually toward maximum openness, honesty, trust, authenticity, patience, receptivity, sharing, freedom and fun. I also include specific ways to augment these goals in action. What I've found is that almost all of my clients very much value this addendum – it opens up a new space in the relationship for us both to enjoy our work together and also to maximize creative success in our ventures.

In this light, what I aim for with my interns is that they always feel they can approach me and tell me anything – with zero judgment from me. It often takes a bit of time for them to get comfortable with this new sense of openness, because it's relatively rare. There's still so much mistrust, apprehension and distance in most business relationships. Hopefully the mentor-intern relationship we're talking about here will begin to reverse this negative situation.

In many ways the mentor/intern relationship is a mature adult expression of the parent-child relationship, with not only a difference in age and experience but also with a deeper shared sense of equality. I want to meet interns where they are at and stand shoulder-to-shoulder with them as we explore the wonderful world of business together.

From the beginning I strive to discover what the intern wants to get out of this work experience – what they want to develop in themselves, and what might get in the way of their being successful with this intent. As the internship begins, I usually have them write some pages expressing their passions, their intentions, their worries and aspirations. Then all through the internship we schedule periodic 15-to-20-minute calls and talk about their progress in accomplishing their goals. We talk, we listen, we learn and discover together. This is a communication structure designed for steady growth and self-actualization.

> *When I'm doing the talking,*
> *I'm not doing the learning.*

J.B. Fuqua

Creating Time

The one primary asset a mentor is obviously committing to in an intern relationship is this thing we call time. This invisible commodity is probably the main commodity that business people say they never have enough of. Linear time is of course clearly tangible at the level of a ticking clock or a computer display. And it's a precious commodity that can be wasted all too easily – in fact it slips through our fingers constantly. We can't store time. We can't fully grasp time. And we can't produce more of it.

So – how is an over-busy manager in a company going to find any time at all to focus their attention toward an intern?

Likewise, how is an intern going to learn to manage their time to their best advantage?

In business as everywhere else, time is gauged by focused attention. I agree to give my full attention to you for a certain time period – that's the basic foundation of employment the world over. You show up at 9 am and you leave at 5 pm and while you're busy at work, you promise to devote your mind's full focused attention where your boss expects you to. Isn't that the general idea of employment?

For an internship to succeed, this element of focused attention needs to be openly addressed. Your hosting company is expecting you to focus your full at-work time in directions that further the company – and simultaneously, you as an intern are expecting your host company to provide someone who dedicates a certain amount of time regularly focusing on you. If this underlying (and often unspoken) agreement isn't adhered to, then either the company is going to feel taken advantage of or the intern is going to feel neglected. Neither of these outcomes is desirable.

And there's also another primary element in this time equation. In addition to their existing work schedule, your mentor is agreeing not only to focus their attention on you regularly, but also to be empathically present for you. That's what's really going on in any nurturing relationship. And if your mentor doesn't provide this 'loving attention' then you as an intern are getting far less out of the experience than you may have expected.

Yet another key element in this 'focused time' equation is the willingness to commit. A mentor who only has good intentions will only serve you so far. You're going to need a mentor who agrees to be there for you – and actually shows up during the designated time frame, and isn't 'too busy.' This now brings us to something I consider the foundation of business itself – working conscientiously with a calendar to ensure that everyone agrees on how company time is going to be spent.

This is one of the main things managers are paid to do – they manage time. They consider how much time they have available in a day or week, they decide what projects have top priority – and then they commit to spending a certain amount of time to fulfilling each of the most important items on their to-do list. This means creating a certain amount of dedicated time that's to be spent focusing fully toward that manager's intern.

What happens when someone focuses their loving attention in your direction? Most likely you light up emotionally, your mood brightens and you also focus your attention back – in this case toward your manager. This act of mutual devoted focusing is what generates any encounter, any relationship, any team effort. As soon as one person shifts their focus away from the other person, the energetic connection is lost – and time and energy are no longer fully building that relationship.

One of the truly mystifying features of human consciousness is that we have the ability to zone out, to lose our focus of attention and basically not be present while still being physically present. It's not enough to set aside 15 minutes for a morning call with your mentor. You also must commit to maintaining an alert focus of attention on that person's presence, and on the exchanges that ensue. This might seem obvious and easy – but in reality it's not.

Far too many students have developed negative attention habits, for instance when their teacher was boring them, or the topic itself bored them. They might still look like they're absorbing what's being said, but in fact most of their focus is on internal flows of ideas that might not be related at all to the topic at hand. These 'fade out' habits need to be observed while you're in college and consciously overcome if you want to succeed in business.

We all know the line: "Sorry, I don't have time for you now" or "Not now, I'm busy." Many parents push away their children hundreds of times with lines like these because the parent's just too busy to focus on the child. As a result we tend to have a negative reaction to the whole process of asking for attention. However, in your intern role you do have the right, and the need, to ask for the attention you've been promised.

At any stage in your business career, if you're not getting the focused attention and dedicated time you need, it's important to speak up! Through practice while interning, you can develop this inner power and confidence to demand the fulfillment of all agreements related to your daily allotment of time. This will assist you in fulfilling your work commitments. Otherwise, resentment will build up and things will turn sour. Often people mismanage their time and simply fail to meet their agreements. When this happens, you must kindly point this out and find your way clearly onto their calendar so that you get the time and attention you deserve.

It's often said that time flies when you're having fun, and it's true. When you're engrossed in a project, time seems to disappear entirely – which is exactly what you want. You still need to be responsible for scheduled meetings and deadlines but aside from that you can let go of time altogether. That's when creativity explodes, new ideas pop into mind and great work gets done. Time is not an issue anymore, you're functioning in what's often called eternal time – you're in the flow ... in the zone.

> *The great mistake is to anticipate*
> *the outcome of the engagement.*
> *Let nature take its course*
> *and strike at the right moment.*

Bruce Lee

Small Bits Of Time

Related to effective time management, I'd like to share with you one of the best pieces of advice I ever received – one of those special nuggets that suddenly appeared out of nowhere and became a permanent part of how I approach life. I was in line at the old student center, waiting to get a treat before going to study. My teaching assistant from East Asian Studies was behind me in line. He saw my impatience and said to me simply: "You know, Rob, the key to college is to use the small bits of time."

I realized immediately that he was right – I wasn't using those five minutes waiting in line for anything at all. I was just fuming about the long line and otherwise not focusing on anything productive. I was entirely wasting this bit of time because I didn't consider a small amount of time worth anything to me.

If you observe a day in your life and count up all the short units of time that you have had available, but that you unwittingly wasted because you didn't think they were of any value, how much time do you think you'd find you wasted in a day? Multiply that by 365 and you'll find that you let slip away many whole days each year. These bits of time add up – moments that you could have used productively if you entertained a different perspective on managing your time.

What can you accomplish in just two minutes of focused attention while on hold for this or that service? What progress might you make if you filled your five-minute 'open times' with focused inner activity? The list of things you might accomplish here and there is quite long – and different for each of us.

For instance, if you're waiting in line or on the phone for just one minute, you could just zone out and not focus on anything in particular – or you could use that bit of time to regain your present-moment awareness. Mindfulness training is all about doing this. You shift your attention fully to your breaths coming and going. Doing this tunes you into your whole-body presence. This focal shift in and of itself has been proven to improve overall health, reduce stress, and make you feel better. In just one minute you can raise your sense of personal power, make heart contact, and relate at higher levels, thereby clearing your mind for new insights.

The basic rule, as I mentioned before, is that if you're not self-aware, you're in many ways simply not here at all. There's no-one home for other people to relate with and there's nothing worthwhile happening inside your own mind or body. When you quickly shift into present-moment alertness while on hold, the couple more minutes you might have to wait become an opportunity to focus on a top-priority challenge or project with a brighter mindset.

Furthermore, breakthrough insights often come flooding into our minds when we temporarily quiet our thoughts, focus on our whole-body presence, and then tune in to new ideas that might pop up. In fact, new ideas can pop into the mind only when we open up a bit of inner space for them to manifest. Think of what happens in the shower – first you relax, tune in to your body and enjoy the soothing sensations. Your thoughts become temporarily quiet. In that moment the solution to a question or problem can effortlessly appear.

In parallel, when you finish a phone call five or ten minutes early, this is an ideal time to discipline your mind and remember what's most important to focus on, and then spend that bit of time advancing your thoughts on the topic. It's all about taking responsibility for where you focus your attention each and every moment of your day.

I'm not saying you need to be in business-work gear all the time. What I am saying is that to get the most out of your internship, and all of life for that matter, it's important not to zone out but rather to consciously stay in the zone. Even if all you do is enjoy this moment – that's great. Just be sure to make the most of all your small bits of time.

Are you familiar with being in the zone? Can you remember moments when you were entirely in the flow, doing something you felt passionately about, and losing all sense of time as you immersed yourself in the project? And can you imagine in the near future letting yourself shift into this seemingly-magical state of consciousness where you're busy accomplishing something but not really working – feeling playful, having great fun, thoroughly enjoying each new moment ...

Chapter Nine

PRODUCTIVELY SEEKING

~~~~~~~~~~~~~~~~~~~~~~~

The probability that we may fail in the struggle
ought not to deter us from supporting
a cause we believe to be just.

Abraham Lincoln

If you have been looking for more ideas on how to find an internship – this is the chapter. But before you start that process, you're going to want to examine your integrity. It is the foundation of productivity and everything you want to build.

Earlier we talked about the universal virtues that the whole world runs on. Included in that list was the virtue of integrity, which means honoring your word and actually doing what you say you'll do. So many people fudge on little things that add up over time – like continually running a bit late, for instance. They're always behind time – and they say that it's just how they are, that it's their nature or something. But in reality, being habitually late is a negative habit of not honoring your word, not doing what you agree to – and this can be changed.

If you deal with being late regularly, or something similar to this, then it's imperative to confront it, especially in work situations. If you don't, then your words won't be valued. People need to know that you're reliable, that you can manage your time well enough to be trusted. It's also a matter of respect. If you truly honor other people and their time commitments, then you're going to discipline yourself so that you're on time.

The key to this kind of discipline is how you manage your calendar. If you write in your calendar that you're going to be somewhere at a set time, then you need to commit to and honor that agreement. You need to act as if your integrity is at stake with each entry you make in your calendar. Be realistic. It's wise not to overbook your calendar. Account for things you might miss or underestimate, like your travel time and unexpected interruptions. My intern Mohammed made this comment:

"While there is certainly value in a classroom education, the professional and time-management skills needed in a work environment are best practiced during an internship. My internship exposed me to challenges and insights of working in a professional setting early on in my career."

When you arrive to begin your internship, I do hope you'll hold this 'time factor' in mind. As an intern manager I definitely watch my interns to see if they are trustworthy timewise. Are they respectful of my time? Will they show integrity with the clients I assign them to – or are they unreliable when it comes to time management? By showing integrity in terms of time management, you demonstrate your integrity overall.

For many of you, at first this won't be easy. Perhaps you're someone who rushes here and there. Perhaps you tend to forget appointments until it's too late to get there on time. Perhaps you get so engrossed in your work that you lose touch with time altogether. No matter – deal with it! And the best way to do that is to take your calendar seriously.

Every time you agree to a time frame, fully commit to that agreement. Also practice leaving some space in your calendar, rather than overbooking. You can always fill those open bits of time, as we mentioned, with reflective, meditative and other productive moments.

> *You will survive anything*
> *if you live your life from*
> *the point of view of truth.*

Oprah Winfrey

Effectively Reaching Out

I'd also like to talk a bit further about how best to reach out to companies you're interested in approaching. For a first step you'll find that at many universities you can very easily go to your career services office and look through all the internships listed. You can also look and see if any of your university's alumni groups are hosting events for interns. Focusing on reaching out to alumni tends to be most worthwhile since you have something in common. So check to see if any alums have volunteered to offer their services for career networking – and if so, jump in and reach out to them.

I'm often asked if moving through online channels and blindly applying online is ever effective. My response usually is that, by and large, you can't expect much from this approach to finding an internship. However, I encourage you to go ahead and do this step anyway because … you never know. But make sure you do it with the right frame of mind, which is that you're not going to put eight hours a day into it. Give this approach maybe half an hour a day and set your expectations appropriately low for the kind of result you'll get from this effort. Moving through the process is valuable mostly because it will get you focused and probably lead you to discovering several companies that pique your interest.

When you become genuinely interested in interning at a particular company, I recommend using LinkedIn to see who works there that you may have a connection to. Then research each person as much as you can (where did they come from, how long have they been at the company, what skills have they developed, what have they accomplished, who does it seem they mostly interact with) before you actually contact them.

Once you are ready to reach out, contact them not only because you're looking for an internship. Authentically approach them looking for advice and assistance as you strive to learn more about opportunities in their industry. From that beginning point, things might open up naturally and effortlessly. Maybe get a sense of what their role is with the interns or entry-level hires at their own firm. If they are involved they can share about working with prior interns. That can really open up the conversation.

Strive toward being relaxed and feeling 'in the zone' just before you phone or video call. Practice flowing with whatever spontaneously opens up in a conversation, rather than trying to manipulate the conversation. If nothing seems to open up with this person, then ask for two or three people they know in the industry who are alumni and would be willing to share with you their perspective of the industry.

Your primary goal is to get conversations flowing with people in your preferred industry. Express your honest passion and also your interest in the actual person you're approaching. Again, authenticity and transparency should be your guiding principles for making a significant connection. As in so many other aspects of life, your success in engaging with someone in a company will come from intentionality and effort, your liveliness along with a sprinkle of pure luck. Throughout, you'll find that your attitude (positive and respectful), your appearance (how you express your intentions), and your preparation (research) will carry you along.

In sum: You don't necessarily want to approach people by saying "Hi, I'm looking for a job, I'm contacting you for an internship." You want to say honestly that you're interested in their industry and want to learn more about their company. Ask politely: "Might you have time for an informational interview?" In the back of their minds, the person you're reaching out to may sense that you have an interest in working in their company in some way. But leave it for them to offer up what they can and want to out of the goodness of their heart for a young person.

What's solid in this approach is that in truth, you are honestly looking for advice. This expression of your interest can then easily lead to other things. At some point you can say you've already formally applied online and ask if they could perhaps assist you in that process – or if they might refer you to someone else in the industry whom they're friends with, so that you can continue to learn? As I mentioned before, be sure to send them a hand-written note thanking them for their assistance. That will set you apart.

In your thank-you note, acknowledge them for their time. Thank them for sharing with you what they know about their industry – the leaders, the current challenges, the direction of the industry's future and how it's evolving. Emphasize what you spoke about together.

Here's a sample note that I received from one of my interns:

> *I just wanted to write you a letter to express my gratitude for your time and advice. Yesterday, I got the amazing opportunity to be interviewed by you, and I couldn't be happier that I decided to apply to your internship for the winter! No matter the outcome of the interview, thank you for already helping me learn so much and grow in my professional skills.*
>
> *I know that as a successful professional, you don't really need to reach out to students, take time to create new opportunities, or spend hours on the phone getting to know us. But, the fact that you would do that means so much to me. As a student who doesn't have a very clear picture of what I want to do in the future, I'm extremely thankful to*

connect with people like you who genuinely want to help and share your experience.

Thank you so much for sharing your book list with me, giving me feedback on my interview, and giving me guidance with respect to the future. As I said, regardless of internship status, I'm so thankful I can now have you as a contact. Thank you again for making yourself available, despite being extremely busy with Agile Rainmakers, your family, and I'm sure much more.

Have an amazing holiday season, and I hope you and your family are safe and healthy!

Thank you again. Sincerely ...

Another thing to hold in mind is to always be listening and looking for what the other person might want to learn, where you can be of service to them. Look to see what you might offer them, not just how you can be served. The idea here is to begin to develop a mindset of giving rather than just taking. You'll be surprised at what will unexpectedly open up in your life if you reach out with a mindset of giving rather than taking.

You'll need to prepare for this – so take time each day to pause ... and reflect on what you have to offer people you're interacting with. And reflect on your readiness to be of help in your chosen industry. What do you have to give, and are you ready to give it? On a daily basis, actively develop this "I'm here to be of assistance" attitude.

Playing The NO Game

Here's a suggestion that might make a real difference for you. Many students are afraid to get rejected – but if you don't put yourself out there and receive some 'no's, you're never going to get a 'yes'. So I recommend perhaps playing a game – aim to receive 100 rejections! Keep researching, keep reaching out, keep putting yourself in position to receive a 'yes' or a 'no'. That's the only way you're going to move ahead.

The idea is to welcome your rejections. They reflect your long-term intent, your ongoing effort, your dogged determination to ultimately get the 'yes' you're determined to manifest. This is a tried-and-true path to success – and people on the other end will respect you for your determination. They will also be inspired by your unflappable positivity when you get a 'no'.

Determination is a prime quality that employers are looking for. If you passionately want to work in a particular industry, you'll ultimately be rewarded for expressing your passion. I remember playing this "100 No's" game about twenty years ago. The game was to get 100 'no's in my job search. I got to seven 'no's – and then the eighth was a 'yes' – and it was exactly the job I was hoping for. The first seven 'no's were all less promising opportunities!

The process of internship-hunting can either build you up or wear you down. Which do you prefer? It's up to you. Your attitude and approach to that process determines which of the two alternatives happens to you. Luckily your attitude and approach are variables that you yourself can fully control. And note that 'how you choose to see' the search process will determine how you feel toward that process – and how you feel will determine your level of motivation, your clarity of intent, and finally, how long it takes to achieve your success in the intern search.

As we've said several times in this book, it's highly rewarding to take plenty of time to pause, look inward a few moments, and without judgment observe your reflex feelings, your ingrained attitudes, your moment-to-moment behavior or lack of action. If you see that you're feeling anxious about rejections, deal with that anxiety by getting to the source of what is so anxiety-producing – and get yourself into actions that will help you decondition old apprehensions about being rejected. Get yourself a bunch of rejections and you'll see that they don't damage you at all. In fact they can inspire you.

Each 'no' that you receive reflects your determination to get a 'yes'. As long as you're growing, learning, exploring and connecting you're doing great. Remember that a process is just that – something unfolding step by step over time. So give yourself time. Start looking for and researching intern positions early. And like I said a few pages ago, begin to live by your calendar. Set aside a certain amount of time each week on your calendar for intern research – and stick to that commitment like your life depends on it.

The reality you're dealing with is that there are more students seeking really great internships than there are great internships. For instance, for a one-month winter internship 60 resumes landed my way for two openings. Build into your game plan the possibility that you won't find a top-notch internship. It can happen. As long as you're exercising your muscle to succeed in general, the time you spend searching for a great internship will be useful and valuable.

Also – perhaps you'll go do something quite different than intern for the summer – or you'll end up in a bothersome intern situation that teaches you loads about work and life. You can never tell where things will lead – and perhaps getting all those 'no's will be a blessing in retrospect because they left you available for some entirely new opportunity that you'd never have anticipated.

The key is to actively program yourself to stay positive. That's your primary challenge. Remember that any engagement with your chosen industry is a positive. Perhaps after a month of focusing on one industry, you might realize you're in fact more interested in another industry – that's progress too.

You're on a great life adventure and you really have little idea where you're going to end up. That's wonderful, your future is wide open! Just keep moving forward. Don't assume that your youthful ego mind already knows what's best. Each time you reach out to someone as a potential employer or mentor, you're taking both a risk and a leap of faith. You don't have to stay immersed in the known – instead you can choose to stay open to discover what awaits you in the unknown.

> *Opportunity is always temporary.*
> *It must be either seized or lost.*
>
> **J.B. Fuqua**

Develop Your Skills

I remember my summer job after freshman year in college. My dad was a doctor and he got me work on the groundskeeping crew at his hospital. Back then I had no idea about getting an internship and I certainly had little interest in a summer engineering job. My parents expected me to not just sit around doing nothing all summer – so I spent three hot and humid months working with a hedger, string trimmer, rake, broom, shovel and whatever other tools they handed me.

During that same summer, knowing my typing skills were limited, I signed up for an evening typing class at our local community college, determined to develop that general skill. Computers weren't as prevalent as they are now and typing was considered mostly a secretarial skill – but I decided to go for it. As a result of three hours of learning and practice two nights a week for six weeks, I got really fast at typing, and that skill has always been a plus ever since.

I also learned a great deal from working on the grounds crew. I got my first taste of having a boss and being on a work team. I learned how good it feels to complete a work assignment, even if it was only raking leaves and making a place look good. I also learned just how good it felt to get my first check! I grew in leaps and bounds during that summer even though it was just a job – not an internship – with no future at all for me. And the most interesting part of that job was learning about my fellow workers. What a bunch of great characters!

Wherever you end up, in a mundane summer job or perhaps an internship that plants seeds for your future career, you're going to learn that each morning when you wake up, you're the one who determines how that day will turn out. You're the one who talks to yourself as you get dressed, saying either "I look forward to whatever comes my way," or "Oh damn, not another laborious day." Realizing that you have this interior choice is perhaps the greatest thing you'll learn during your internship.

As you're eagerly searching for an ideal internship, you'll also want to have your Plan B ready if needed. Have something to fall back on as an alternative job to do for the summer – something that will enrich you in some way. The last thing you want for your summer is to have nothing productive to do. Doing nothing will in fact move you backward.

And like I said before, even if you're stuck raking leaves and mowing lawns and weeding around hedges, your mind can either fight against your situation and learn nothing, or open to new experiences and insights. Who knows, those challenges might suddenly make sense for a future career – you might think of a new way to compost fiber, or invent a novel way to organize labor more efficiently. You might have a realization about management and workers that you'll take into an entirely different industry where you're running a hundred employees in a new way. Every moment's an opportunity to discover what you're really interested in. There's no better way to get clear about what you like to do, than from time to time doing something that you don't really like.

There are no limits.
There are only plateaus,
and you must go beyond them.

Bruce Lee

Spending Free Time Wisely

Here's a good question: What is it you (your mind and body) are usually yearning to do in your free time? The answer to this question will tell you a lot about your interests in work and life. I personally spend a lot of my free time staying in touch with friends by text, email and phone. I even created a newsletter just to keep in touch. When I first moved to Chicago I spent a ton of time on weekends reaching out to old friends and colleagues. I don't do that as much now, being settled and married with kids – but I still know deeply that I'm someone for whom enduring friendships are important.

Half of us are introverts and half extroverts. The more introverted a person is, the more important it is to make the effort to stay in touch, to network, to be interactive. In most endeavors, teamwork is going to be important for success. For instance I'm a fairly good writer but I couldn't just jump in and write a book like this one on my own. Instead I used my networking and social skills to reach out and collaborate with a life-long writer of similar books. Together we possess all the talent and experience needed to complete a project we couldn't manifest alone.

Of course there are a lot of jobs that are done solo, where people can be productive and excel and do the best they can.

One of the fundamental things to know about yourself is if you prefer working alone or on a team. Can you work alone enjoyably for long periods of time, or do you need regular social interaction? Knowing this basic fact about your work and play preferences will tell you a lot about the kinds of opportunities you should be seeking.

Perhaps we might pause here so that you can actively make a list of what you like and don't like to do with your free time. Get a notepad or computer or whatever you prefer to take notes on, and begin to fill out two columns, one titled LIKES and the other DISLIKES – or STRONG INTEREST and LOW INTEREST. Don't overthink this, just quickly write down what comes to mind as you imagine doing each item. Try to get at least a dozen items in each column.

> ## LIKES   DISLIKES

And now, once you have your two lists you can pause, maybe walk around a bit, tune in to your breathing and your bodily presence – get some distance from the lists.

And now go back and look at the two lists again – and see what insights come to your mind about your preferences in life. Make changes and additions as you want to. Then contemplate how you can match your general interests with possible career choices – and also match your 'low interests' with careers that you don't want to pursue.

And to end this process, write down your ideal job or career. What can you envision doing on a daily basis for years that would be truly satisfying? Take some time to create your ideal job description.

And ... once every couple of weeks, return to this list of what you really like to do and your related job description. Feel free to rewrite and evolve your description of your ideal job. You'll find that this ongoing process can work wonders in aiming your attention and actions toward fulfillment in your career.

Pause & Reflect

~~~~~~~~~~~~~~~~~~~~~~~~

Chapter Ten

BEING MENTORED

~~~~~~~~~~~~~~~~~~~

Be to her virtues very kind;
Be to her faults a little blind.

Matthew Prior

I've learned that I really enjoy mentoring people. This is a wonderful thing. It's a form of volunteering that can be one of the most rewarding activities in life. It's the opposite of staying habitually self-absorbed. You put yourself out there beyond your ego needs. In the process of helping someone outside your personal bubble you let go of your fixed views and make new discoveries. Often in the process you'll find your future opening up in rewarding directions.

When we focus our attention toward the needs of others rather than on ourselves, we put ourselves in position to see the world in ways we never would've considered if we hadn't volunteered to be of service to another. Spending time as a volunteer moves us forward in life. As we give, we definitely also receive – and we learn to stay mentally flexible and adaptable. We also rediscover that it feels good to do good.

Serving as an intern can be seen very similarly. You come into a company for a fairly short predetermined period of time. You help out where you can, you volunteer to do whatever needs doing – and you reap multiple benefits. You don't make a pile of money but you learn through experience whether or not you like the environment, whether you like the work, and if you enjoy the people who do this type of work.

I usually advise interns to pay attention to the clients and compare them to each other looking from many different perspectives. What aspects of each client are exemplary and what aspects aren't, and why? Who seem to be most self-aware and emotionally grounded? As an intern, set a goal to find someone successful who's willing to give their perspective in a nurturing way. By doing so, that positive role model may open up new vistas in many dimensions. One intern made this related comment:

"Having good mentors in a workplace is now very important to me, it's become the factor that I consider most heavily in applying for a new position."

You can approach your college experience the same way. For instance, the therapist I met with a number of times at Princeton was absolutely brilliant. I learned a lot from him. I also learned from many of the teaching assistants at Princeton. They could cut right to the deeper insights of a topic. I also knew classmates who were brilliant. The trick is not to compete with them, but to be open and appreciate them fully so that learning takes place. That's also the essence of a friendship, yes? Be open to receive – and of course share what you have to offer.

There's also the whole notion of realizing what you truly need as opposed to what you simply want. What do you need to have in order to feel happy, satisfied and fulfilled in life? It's so important to get clear on that as early as you can because it'll make everything else flow so much easier. As spiritual teachers (and the Rolling Stones) regularly say, usually what we need is far less than what we want. Somehow, paradoxically, when we need less we end up with a lot more of what we truly want.

Sadly, far too often when we struggle to get what we think we need in life, it ends up not being all that satisfying. Ever have that happen to you? You're happy for a moment or a day – but then you feel empty and frustrated and so you start looking for something new to try to get, to satisfy you.

Once you get honest with yourself and observe your chronic habits of running constantly after some new thing to satisfy you, finally you can begin to free yourself. You can look and feel in your heart and in your gut what you really need. And when you do get what you truly need – ahh! Then anything above and beyond that is just an extra, not essential for your happiness.

All of this seems so obvious and too easy – but in reality we were all programmed as kids to think that something 'out there' separate from us is going to satisfy us. We know this isn't true from experience but still this way of thinking persists. We're locked into that chronic pattern. That is what much of advertising and sales are all about – convincing us that we need to get something or buy something in order to feel good.

Life actually works exactly the other way around. One way or another we must learn to generate our own sense of inner happiness, regardless of our circumstances. We must realize that we're the only one in control of how we feel each new moment. We always have the choice to react negatively and feel bad, or to respond to whatever comes at us in a way that lets us feel good.

Exercising choice is a very high level of living. That's what we want to strive toward – a self-sustaining emotional stance in life where our happiness is not a function of what we want or acquire. It's a function of how well we ourselves manage our inner realms of being. I've got nothing against material wealth and comfort and so forth. But I don't advise placing your entire sense of worth and fulfillment on the size of your bank account. With that perspective on life you can minimize worries and maximize the pure pleasure of getting up each morning and going eagerly off to work.

You can approach your internship with that same attitude. In choosing an intern position, it seems best to decide beforehand what minimum circumstances you're willing to accept to enjoy the experience. Use your personal judgment in terms of what will work for you. Be in communication with the people you're considering interning with so that you can manage your expectations.

Also, do what you can from your end to make the internship match what you're seeking. Value most highly the people you're going to be relating with. Fully prepare yourself for the reality you're going to plunge into for a summer, a winter, a semester, or a year. If you become confident that you can sustain an inner sense of joy and contentment regardless of your externals, then you can relax into your internship.

Pragmatically, once you've gone and made your decision and committed to a company, be sure that you ask to be in communication regularly with someone in the company. Let's say you were accepted in February and your internship doesn't start until June. Be proactive and say, "Is it possible every six weeks or so for me to connect with my manager on the phone or video call for half an hour, to keep up to date on what's happening in the company?" Feel free to also ask for any books or other resources that will help you keep in tune with the industry.

Then when June comes, you'll have oriented yourself, picked up the company language, developed some tacit knowledge and already have a little bit of a relationship. You'll be able to hit the ground running on the company side. Like I said, be sure to ask for what you feel you need as preparation. You might ask: "Do you have any books, articles or industry newsletters I should look at that'll help me make the most out of the summer? I'd love any ideas you have. Is there anything I could research?" It's hard for a company person to say no to those kinds of requests and you'll quickly create a good connection.

You can apply this same logic and strategy toward alumni from your university. Research who's currently employed in your desired industry and reach out to them. Express your interest and your eagerness to learn more about what they do. You'll very possibly come across someone who has a natural eagerness to be a mentor. Who knows what might develop –

but the first step is yours. You must make the effort. You must also feel an authentic interest. Then flow with that eagerness to engage and learn from people already succeeding in the industry that excites you.

As in all things, like I mentioned before, if you're overly self-centered you're not going to succeed. So instead, practice being more interested in what other people are wanting. Explore how you might fulfill their needs while at the same time fulfilling your own. Win-win works everywhere. Begin to figure out what corporate mentors and intern managers are themselves seeking. Are you willing and eager to enter into a mentor/mentee relationship with an older industry person? Who are they looking for? Can you fill that role?

Honestly, if you can't, don't take the position. Perhaps you come to realize after doing this reflective analysis of the intern role that you're not suited for it at all. That's perfectly fine. Don't force yourself to intern if you don't want to. You're free as a college student to change your mind, to change course, and to entertain different possibilities for your future. If you follow your heart, your passion, and your natural attractions before you get a job, your whole future will manifest itself in satisfying outcomes. It will.

A good mentor will feel a natural supportive attraction to you. They'll be able to stand in your shoes, see from your perspective, and think with you. They'll be willing to honestly share their own challenges with you. They'll offer you something quite rare – a window of reality through which to see their industry. If you can find a mentor who's willing to share with you what they're dealing with, this will prove invaluable. You'll get a real sense of what it would be like for you to advance into that industry.

*You get in life what you have
the courage to ask for.*

Oprah Winfrey

Take The Leap

I'd like to talk a bit about risk-taking. When you decide to find a good internship, you're definitely taking a leap into the new. You're risking getting rejected, you're risking getting assigned to a bad mentor and having a negative experience. You're plunging into unexpected situations where you might fail or get damaged emotionally in some way, or find you've been misled into situations where you don't belong. Taking risks is, well, risky. There are many potential downsides – but having the courage to accept and deal with risks is always a necessary stance in exploring any new venture.

If you think you know what an internship is going to be like, and you think it might (emphasis on "might") have negative aspects and so you say no to the position – then you avoid the risk but you also avoid a possibly rewarding experience. As you have probably heard before: "Nothing risked, nothing gained – and nothing still remains."

If you're hesitant to take risks, if in particular you feel anxious about risking an internship experience, then I advise the following process to overcome your hesitancy. Take some very small risks at first. Decondition your fears little by little. For instance, risk taking just the first step – that of looking online to see what internships are available.

Risk focusing your power of attention gently and tentatively in that general intern direction. Then once you see that there was no danger in doing that step, risk a bit more by going to your university Career Center and talking to the people who work there about your general interests. Look up what's available through their help. Stay aware of your hesitancy – and how it drops away when you experience the safe and valuable reality of making that step.

Also, when it comes time to apply for an interview, you might want to start by approaching a company that isn't at all on your list. Do a test run with them – and when you have your interview, just relax and be yourself … and see what happens. Risk being authentic! Get comfortable with yourself and the general interview situation. Break the ice. Get that first interview behind you.

Also start taking small risks in other aspects of your everyday life. Begin to notice what you're afraid to attempt and explore – and find a small situation to risk in that direction. Maybe go to a store and ask for a discount not being offered. Just experiment here and there and see how it feels. Embrace that feeling of risking, of perhaps even looking a little foolish – and let those lingering fears from your past dwindle and be gone. Doing this as a conscious discipline for a few weeks or months can quite dramatically change your life for the better. You'll risk more and a predictable result will be you'll gain more.

It might sound strange to say this, but I strongly recommend that you follow the path of risking and failing early and often in your life. Learn how to deal with failure. You're going to fail a lot if you're on your unique path to success. If you want to reduce your failures later on, work through as many of those mistakes as you can when you're in your teens and twenties.

You can consciously learn how to manage that experience of failure. Failure is not something to fear and avoid. It's an exploratory adventure to embrace. It's what free play is all about – and free play is the font of new discovery. By experiencing failure a number of times you'll develop a resilience that will serve you beautifully on many fronts in your career. A recent intern put it this way:

"Some of my most valuable moments of growth in my internship experience occurred when I put away the fear of failure and confronted areas where I felt less confident. Failing and learning from failure has allowed me to garner valuable experience, and develop greater confidence in crucial skills I'd need to advance in my career."

In the business world there are two things that you can do with risk. Either you can avoid it, or you can manage it. College is a great time to learn to manage risk and stop avoiding the failure that often accompanies it. The only risks you want to avoid in college are the ones that will genuinely harm you. Beyond that, each time you have the opportunity to try something new, go ahead and bravely take the leap into exploring that experience.

Especially be brave and eagerly embrace the risk of looking bad, of being embarrassed, of stumbling and being judged. If you don't risk looking bad, you're going to miss out on so many experiences in life that could teach you something essential for success later on. If you don't go for it in life you're going to miss out on adventures, friendships and possibly romance and other deeply rewarding encounters. Everyone has their inherited and childhood hesitations. College is the perfect time and place to put hesitations aside and dive into the unknown!

We've all been hurt and we don't ever want to be hurt again, do we? But if we don't risk again we remain stuck. Of course, don't be foolish and risk serious damage – but otherwise, dive in every time you have an opportunity. Get banged around and discover that you're stronger than you thought you were, both physically and emotionally. Every risk you take, whether you succeed or fail, will teach you important lessons in life. College is such a great chance to move through a lot of risky situations without serious consequences. Do this and you'll be ahead of the game when you graduate.

Nothing in life is to be feared,
it is only to be understood.

Marie Curie

Chapter Eleven

FOCUSED LOVING ATTENTION
~~~~~~~~~~~~~~~~~~~~~

A moment of self-compassion
can change your entire day.
A string of such moments can
change the course of your life.

Christopher Germer

As I mentioned, I had 60 students apply to intern in my consultant firm during a winter break. I interviewed 13 of them, and I took each interview very seriously. I found that I felt a deep connection with about half of the group, and then I hired four of them. I didn't yet know what I'd do with those four. I originally wanted only two interns for that winter break month. But I was confident that, with my basic structure and design for the winter internship, we had in hand a compass to guide us through the experience, with the details allowed to unfold day by day.

What I did do with these four new interns, as I do with all my interns, was openly commit to being their trustworthy guide at a deep level. I knew that they mostly wouldn't need me to teach them how to code Java or whatever for a client. They probably wouldn't need any pragmatic training from me –

they already knew most of that in spades because they were very diligent, responsible, conscientious students.

But what they would definitely need me to do for them was this: they'd need me to take time to focus loving attention toward them personally, and to do so regularly. They would need me to pause and hear them out without judging or interrupting them. Rather than dominating them as an overlord, I'd need to strive to relate with them as equals – and let them know that in my eyes they're entirely okay, both as up-and-coming business successes and more importantly as worthwhile upstanding human beings.

To fulfill my role as mentor and guide, I readily committed myself to certain actions and inactions. One action I always make is to inform and get buy-in from my entire family about my commitment to the interns. I assess how much of my family time will be spent focusing on the interns, and I make sure my family members are okay with this. In general I feel the interns add depth to our family life even if they never meet each other.

One thing that I promise is not to day-trade, which would distract me from the interns. I also promise to set aside dedicated one-on-one time for a weekly personal talk with each of my interns. This is time to ask how they're doing with what they're working on – and also to allow them the freedom to share at deeper levels if they choose to. I have a set of questions I go through every week with each intern, so that they can see how they're evolving steadily in their attitudes, expectations and feelings.

As their manager I also have daily scheduled conversations with the group of interns, so that they know I'm fully on their side. I let them know quite often that I want them to win – and I consciously design their assignments to ensure a win. Also, cooperation rather than competition is the atmosphere I encourage at work. Why? Because like I said earlier, another commitment I make to my interns is that we agree to enjoy working together – and a spirit of cooperation nurtures this sense of enjoyment.

I also purposefully seek a sense of balance on the intern teams I bring together in my company. I do my best to have an equal number of men and women. I'm not dogmatic about this and I appreciate the broad spectrum of female-male uniqueness in human sexual identity. But I'm also aware of the importance of energetic balance on a team, and aim to create this balance. I also aim to have my interns aware of its presence.

I strive to have a balance in terms of academic majors and interests. For example on that winter intern team, two were financial engineer majors, one was computer science and one was political science. With that diversity they could naturally experience new perspectives from each other.

Young people usually come into new business situations with a spirit of competition, assuming that that's just how companies operate. I'm not against colleagues striving to be the best. But mostly in healthy work situations, I do find compassionate cooperation a stronger road to success than compulsive competition. I regularly reinforce the notion of self-awareness in this regard, encouraging excellence while also emphasizing cooperative learning. I hope to show my interns by example how to be supportive of each other and how to value the unique power of teamwork.

For me, such underlying considerations are fundamental to the spirit a mentor strives to awaken while working with interns. I'm well aware that this spirit of harmonious relating is all too often missing in intern programs. I hope that this book and its parallel text for intern mentors and managers will help companies shift into a more uplifting approach to sponsoring internships.

I would rather live in a world
surrounded by mystery
than live in a world so small that
my mind could comprehend it.

Harry Emerson Fosdick

Wise Actions During The Interim

Once you've done your interviews and been accepted by a company you prefer – from then on, until you're walking in the door of your intern assignment (or starting online) there are a few obvious but important steps you'll want to make. Along with communicating regularly with your intern manager, and studying the industry diligently, you'll want to see who you can contact for specific advice regarding that industry. A good idea is to reach out to those you interviewed with to thank them again for their time and let them know where you ended up. Remember that each of these new contacts could be important for you down the line. You are building your network.

The more you focus time and attention toward your upcoming internship situation, the more control you'll gain regarding how it'll all unfold for you. The more prepared you are on all fronts, the better you'll do. Too many students do almost nothing in this regard during the months between their acceptance in a company and their engagement with that company.

Of course you'll want to keep up your grades and stay fully immersed in college life. Simultaneously, consciously dedicate adequate time in your calendar, each week, to focus ahead to the summer or winter break or the next semester when you'll be off interning. I also encourage you to take time to pause and actively imagine yourself in your intern role.

Take time to see what you can find online to help you dig deeper into the challenges of the industry you're entering. You can set up an automatically-updated Google industry-news report. Also regularly visit your company's website and those of related corporations to stay up to date on how their online presence is evolving. If you do this diligently, then you'll show up for the internship with a sharp sense of the company's current situation and what you'll perhaps be asked to focus on when you get there. You'll also familiarize yourself with the vocabulary and driving concepts of your industry.

*Give me six hours to chop down a tree
and I will spend the first four
sharpening the axe.*

Abraham Lincoln

Successful Transitioning

It's important, before heading off for your internship, that you clear up everything else in your life that might otherwise be a distraction or an obstacle to focusing entirely on your internship. You'll want to show up complete and wide open, ready to focus on what you want to get out of your internship.

To be fully ready, I recommend actively clearing your college plate of remaining obligations, and also spending some time before the semester ends to write down everything you hope to achieve during your internship. Consciously set your compass. Establish a 'goals-lighthouse' that will stand before you, guiding you toward your own definition of success during your internship. And of course make sure that your goals align with your hosting company's goals for your internship.

You're the one who must begin the process of progressively shifting your mindset out of academic modalities and into what I call 'real world' mode. A solid way to make this inner shift is to find a few people you can 'talk shop' with about your chosen industry. Online or in person, locate and talk with people who've recently interned, so that you begin to get a real feel for what's coming. Learn as much as you can about their experiences, and reflect on what could have made their experience even better.

When your last day of school arrives, be prepared for the mundane physical process of moving. You're going to suddenly end your school year or semester, temporarily let go of your identity as a student – and in most cases move physically away from campus. You're going to take a leap and somehow settle into the reality of a new bed and shelter and all the rest. To do this you're going to have to get very pragmatic as you wrap up your school year, put your furniture and things in storage, and line up where you're going to live during your internship.

Given the option, choose to intern in the office, not work remotely. So much is learned by being immersed in that specific office environment. That is the way to pick up all the subtle and not-so-subtle nuances expressed in one-on-one business relationships. Often you'll want to just be quiet and observe. Don't judge or participate too much – just be all ears and learn through observation.

As I mentioned before, do your best to spend more time listening than talking. Your superiors at work will appreciate this relatively humble stance. You'll be showing that you don't consider yourself a know-it-all and also that you're not self-absorbed. Instead you're being impressionable and receptive – you're engaged! Then when the time is right, you'll probably be asked to express what you think.

Like so many transitions in life, making the move from school to work can be quite anxiety-inducing. But you can usually overcome this by actively planning ahead. Be as mindful as you can. Here's the experience of a recent intern:

"After the interview, when I was notified that I'd received my internship offer, a period of relief and excitement was soon followed by anxiety over the new position. In order to use this anxiety productively, I prepared for my start date by taking time to research trends in the industries I was planning to work in. I also made contact and stayed in touch with co-workers I was looking forward to working with."

Anxiety occurs when you worry too much about what the future is going to be like. When you catch yourself worrying about your approaching internship, just shift your focus of attention away from the future. Find something in the present moment that you can do to prepare for your internship. Work steadily at making your transition – don't save it all for the last day or two.

In certain areas you'll need to plan weeks ahead – like where you're going to live during your internship. You'll also want to make sure you set yourself up properly for coming back to campus from your internship. If you think and plan ahead adequately you won't have to fret about what's coming after your internship ends – you'll be prepared.

The best way to predict your future
is to create it.

Abraham Lincoln

Your Intern Bill Of Rights

As an intern you're going to enter a company at a very low position on the totem pole. You'll probably be asked to do some menial tasks, and that's fine. But you also need to sustain your sense of self-respect. You do have a right to be treated fairly and humanely.

For instance, companies shouldn't work you so long each day that you don't get a good night's sleep. Adequate sleep is an obvious but often-overlooked element of success during an internship and throughout one's life. You perhaps caught the biz-news stories about finance firms working their new employees ridiculous hours, up to 100 hours a week. If you're doing menial rote work playing biorobot, crunching numbers and doing entirely non-creative, zero-relationship work, you can keep up such unhealthy schedules for a while. But even then, at some point you'll crash.

Why? Because physiologically the human organism in general requires 7-8 hours of sleep a night. When you get less than that you're going to perform at lower and lower levels over time. You'll make more and more mistakes, and probably get grumpier and short-tempered, even downright neurotic – and in the process of all that, you'll generally fail. Sleep deprivation is a performance killer.

Any manager should know these biological facts. If they push you too hard anyway, they're not good managers. There's been a lot of machismo in the traditional business environment, where everyone was expected to devote their entire lives to the company. People were worked too long and too hard, and in the process denied all the other dimensions of a good life. If you land in such a stressed-out work environment, you'll be able to sustain a short internship under such inhumane conditions and learn what you don't want for yourself, as we've discussed before. But overall, make sure you honor your own bodily requirements. Nurture your sense of self-love and care enough for your own self that you don't let people abuse you in the name of sacrificing all for the company.

At this core level you deserve to be treated like an equal human being to your manager and colleagues. If you happen to live in a democracy, that's the ideal – equality, fairness, decency and compassion. Begin early to recognize and attract people and companies who share your primary humanitarian values.

No matter what your internship situation might be, you're there to learn at multiple dimensions. Every situation is there to teach you something if you're open and aware in the present moment. Your challenge is to make sure you walk out of that first intern assignment with a sense of fulfillment. Your internship should be a golden time in your life – each internship is a unique adventure that will never come again.

In this regard, during any stage of your internship don't be afraid to reach out to people in the company. You're not going to bother them. Quite the opposite, you're exhibiting interest, enthusiasm, curiosity – and these are key assets. Reach out if you have questions, while feeling comfortable asking for what you need in order to fulfill your intern role. If a company has opened up space for an intern, they're almost surely going to be on your side, not out to sink your boat.

But at the same time, remember not to expect too much from company employees. Of necessity they're focused primarily on the ongoing work they're doing, so do be discrete. Get your work done. Your company will be expecting you to show up, fit in, make a difference where you can, and be receptive. They're also expecting you to be of good humor, helping to raise the spirit of the place rather than drag things down with negative aggravations. You have a responsibility to your team to stay mostly positive, emotionally balanced, polite and considerate. Try to hold this responsibility in mind all the time, even if others don't. You'll be rewarded, I assure you.

How you relate ethically in your intern assignment will probably be an indicator of how you'll operate ethically later on – so pay full attention to your current attitudes and behaviors when it comes to things like social, verbal, sexual and racial conduct. My advice is to avoid conflict where possible – but if you must, stand up for what you feel deep down is right and just and fair. Don't be obnoxious but do be clear and strong where it counts. At core levels you want to always feel good about how you conduct yourself, and about what you stand up for and support in others.

The ultimate measure of a man
is where he stands at times of
challenge and controversy.

Martin Luther King, Jr.

A Company's Intern Intentions

Situations are always changing in a workplace. For instance a whole host of things could shift rapidly between the time you're accepted for an internship and the time you arrive to begin that internship – like who is managing the internship program, what you'll be expected to work on, and even your physical location for the internship. So a couple of weeks before you start, it's a very good idea to give a call or send an email, whichever you prefer, to find out the current status of things in your company. Typically, students are assigned a particular manager or mentor. Do know beforehand who you're reporting to and if you'll be working by yourself or on an intern team.

Also seek clarification on whether a company tends to hire interns as a possible pipeline for future employment or if that is not a given. Don't be pushy about this. Just get a sense of why the company is hiring interns. How do they perceive the payoff? Then decide if that suits your own intentions for interning.

I personally think the current trend toward longer internships that lead to a more permanent position in a company is a good win-win evolution. Things are changing so fast in the business world. The closer you are to those changes the better for you and for the company. Undergrad and business schools are highly valuable in teaching many general skills – but learning to apply those skills beyond standard academic training is what's required for success these days.

The corporate competition for excellent talent is intense. Therefore, companies want to get top students on board with them before their competition does. In this regard the old-time 'apprenticeship' concept is making more and more sense. In general, you'll want to see the internship process as a recruiting tool for corporations. My relatively small company doesn't approach interning this way at this time, but more and more larger companies do.

When you finish an internship, don't be surprised if your company recommends that when you're back finishing your college studies, you also set aside time in your weekly schedule to take a specific course that will train you in particular tools and skills that the company values in a fresh recruit. You might also be offered a part-time work situation with the company, where you fulfill assignments while still on campus. If so, it's probably a good idea to take it. It will keep you in the know and in the running for opportunities that may open up. It's a free option.

Build a foundation of trust
by maintaining confidentiality
and following through on commitments.

Kevin Giulioni

Managing Your Mindset

I want to reiterate how strongly your own prevailing mindset and attitude will influence the outcome of your internship. It's a cliché but still quite true – the feelings, ideas, expectations and underlying vision that you project outward into your work environment will both directly and indirectly impact everyone around you. Improve this basic mindset element and you'll improve your overall progress.

Your internship is an at-work experiment. No one knows how it will turn out, because you yourself are an unknown ingredient which the company can't control beyond the interview-acceptance stage. You're going to be watched to see how you're affecting the company and how you're letting the company affect you. Do you harmoniously fit in? Are you authentic, or are you putting on a show? Do you seek to advance the company, or just to advance your own nascent career? Can you adapt to rapid change and at times be a leader, or are you timid, rigid and inert in changing situations?

Be sure to regularly reflect on this subtle dimension of your internship. Don't just submerge yourself in work. Keep part of your awareness tuned into the larger flow of your experience in the company. Are things moving well for you, or do you see something that could improve? If so, aim to influence the company in positive ways while you're there.

Also, while reflecting on how you're doing in the company that's hosting you, take a bit of time each week to look at how you're spending your off-hours. If you're living at home consider if your family is taking up too much of your attention, and make adjustments where needed. Same with friends, romances and hobbies – are you discovering a healthy balance between them and your workload? If not, then get in communication! Say what you need to them in order to establish a more functional and satisfying balance between work and play.

Be sure not to make the mistake of expecting others to know what is and isn't working for you, without you telling them. Counting on mindreading is a mistake. Communication really is the best tool. One intern reflected on this:

"Through our daily team discussions I was able to hone my communication skills, express my concerns and needs, and boost my confidence in functioning effectively in the workplace."

You might note that many families and teams in such situations find it useful and even essential to schedule half an hour each week for everyone in the household to gather for an informal yet intentional and consequential meeting. Each person gets to 'hold the talking stick' and speak about what they're enjoying, what's bothering them, and what changes they'd like to initiate in the functioning of the group.

Whenever there are conflicts, the group can take time to talk it all through to a win-win resolution. I highly advise using available online tools to facilitate non-violent communication and resolving difficulties. What you need for this process is almost surely out there, so hunt and find it.

You can do this scheduled group meeting with roommates as well. Set a goal to learn early how best to function in group living and work situations. And discover new ways to avoid conflict and maximize teamwork and harmony. We'll have more about this available on our website.

During your internship, steadily work on developing and manifesting your full personal vision of success. Ask yourself:

Do I have enough time to focus on fulfilling my vision?

Do I have the skills I need, plus enough information?

Am I receiving the guidance and leadership I need?

Do I feel anxious and uncomfortable about asking for something that I need in order to succeed with my internship vision?

All of these are important questions. Ask yourself:

When this internship is all over, how do I want to feel about the experience?

How do I want to have grown?

What am I aiming to get out of the time I'll spend interning?

What do I hope to have contributed?

What lasting friendships do I seek to form?

How extensively do I want to network?

When you're finished with your internship, have a list of questions that you're going to ask yourself seriously. Develop this list early on:

Did I stay grounded and balanced during my internship?

Did I roll successfully with what came unexpectedly at me?

How have various people in the company evaluated me?

Have I stayed on course and followed my vision of my internship to final fruition?

You'll want to return often to these and similar questions that you come up with for yourself. It's also effective to write down or type the questions and your answers so that you have an ongoing record of how you're evolving, based on how you respond to the questions at different phases of your internship.

Anybody who succeeds is helping people.
The secret to success is to
find a need and fill it.

Robert H. Schuller

Chapter Twelve

PLAYING THE RIGHT GAME

~~~~~~~~~~~~~~~~~~

Instead of worrying about
what you cannot control,
shift your energy to
what you can create.

Roy Bennett

Companies are always looking for good leaders as well as team players. Where do you personally stand in terms of wanting to be a leader? During your internship you'll have plenty of chances to observe leaders in action, while also considering if you aspire toward a leadership role in your career. For interns, another potent cliché that still rings true is that "If you want to be a good leader, you must first be a good follower."

While interning you'll have many opportunities to develop your 'good follower' skills. You'll be expected to obey orders and fulfill a leader's directives. How do you feel about being a follower? Later on when you're in leadership roles you'll want to reflect on your early intern 'follower' experiences.

While an intern, be sure to observe yourself clearly and honestly, so that you can determine what your unique personality and talents naturally predispose you toward. And when given the chance, even if you don't think you're a natural leader, go ahead and experiment. Take risks and find out what it feels like to lead.

Also practice putting yourself in the company's shoes. Try to engage to the point where you feel that you're an organic part of the corporate whole. Experience how full immersion in an organization feels. Are you in fact a good company person? Can you envision spending much of your career inside the corporate realm, enjoying its security, conformity, structure, power and breadth? Or might you in fact prefer in the long run to have more creative freedom, more intense risks and payoffs, more entrepreneurial adventures?

All of these issues will arise while doing your internship if you manage to stay heads-up and observant of both the company and also your response to that company. Notice continually how well you're doing in terms of self-respect. Is it important to you to impact the company, to contribute something of value? You're probably not going to stay with this company all your work life – but while there, can you honestly participate and produce value? Are you willing to give the team your all? And if not, can you reflect on why, and go to work on that?

The inferior person understands
what is profitable.
The superior person understands
what is right.

Confucius

Journaling For Success

A good tool for all of this is to journal. Every day during your internship, set aside ten minutes or so to write down what worked for you that day, what you struggled with, and what you could have done better. Write down what you intend to do the next day to improve your performance and satisfaction with your work. And make sure when you wake up the next morning to read what you wrote the night before. We'll provide details on how to do this at our website.

Regularly write down what you're going to aim to do differently. This can cover many different levels including mental performance, communication skills, your awareness habits, behavioral patterns and so forth. Make deals with yourself to take risks, explore alternatives. Do all this consciously, with your daily journal entries as visible cues. Even if you note that you're only getting a teeny bit better at something each day, you'll be establishing new habits that will serve you well throughout your life. You'll feel more fully in control of how your internship is progressing every new day. A tiny bit better every day can compound over time to make an enormous difference.

Naturally, there will be things that are going to go off course. As a result you may get frustrated and upset, defensive and confused. Perhaps you're experiencing being belittled by someone, or feel like you're being accused of something, or told that your performance isn't up to snuff. Whatever hits you, fair or unfair, it's going to be your job to manage your emotions.

When things don't go as well as you'd like, or you get feedback that you don't like, you're going to have to act maturely. In those moments, block ingrained defensive reactions from your childhood, and manage to internalize your emotions long enough to reflect on the situation – and then respond with all of your self-confidence and self-control on display. If you can't do that in the moment, don't just react. It's usually much better to excuse yourself and go for a walk, take a breather break – and then come back and be the best you that you can be right then.

What I'm suggesting is that you use your internship as practice for gaining more emotional maturity. Over and over, see if you can bite back your impulse to hit back when you feel unfairly treated or misunderstood. Develop enough inner strength to where you don't need to act immediately – the truth is that you don't. Practice staying quiet when you want to lash out. You're not still dealing with your parents. You're developing new responses to new situations. This is your chance to learn how to channel your emotional charge so as to be harmonious and productive.

And again: use your daily journaling to mark your progress. Even make the effort to write down dialog that occurred that day that may have triggered something in you. Try writing different responses that you might've given in that moment. Learn how to learn from conflict rather than just unconsciously reacting and potentially making things worse.

It's also a good idea to journal about what worked especially well during a day and what you want to acknowledge yourself for having accomplished. There are always positives happening as your growth and development unfolds day by day. Be sure to consciously embrace that too. Share your progress with others. If you do this process consciously, you can transform yourself in directions that you yourself are choosing.

Remember that in this early phase of your career you're an intern. You're just starting – so be good to yourself. No one's expecting you to be a full-time hire with years of experience. They're expecting you to be a college student who's bravely jumping into the workplace. Choose to be modest and your honest self will serve you best. Embrace that feeling of authenticity.

As we talked about earlier, regularly notice how you are talking to yourself about what's happening inside and around you. Listen to the internal dialogs you're creating. What's really behind what you're saying to yourself, and how you're acting? Observe your mental chatter and ingrained reactions without judging them. You'll find that insights come flowing in, and you begin to change for the better.

> *Make peace with your past*
> *so it won't screw up the present.*
>
> **Regina Brett**

Valuing Foolishness

When I look back to my college and early work years I'm amazed at how many foolish things I did, and how seemingly blind I was to a lot of what was going on around me. I was so often caught up in my internal monologue, talking to myself, judging and evaluating myself, rather than being fully engaged with my work and co-workers. What seemed logical to me back then makes me feel embarrassed to admit now.

The important takeaway is that we all tend to do this – but at some point it's really important to learn ways to quiet all the internal chatter so that you can focus more effectively outward on the work at hand. An internship can help you considerably in taking this giant leap outside your own interior monologue.

The way to make this leap is to become self-reflective without becoming self-absorbed or judgmental. Nobody likes to be judged – so why do this same negative thing to ourselves? Instead, before, during and after your internship, I encourage you to stop metaphorically hitting yourself over the head with self-judging accusations. Focus on what you're doing right each new day, and then also take a look at what you might positively act to improve. Let your habitual negativity drop away – and you'll succeed at much higher levels.

If you say to yourself five times in a row, "I'm no good," you'll almost immediately start feeling that way – dull, depressed, worthless. And of course you won't perform well if this is your predominant attitude about yourself. But if you say five times to yourself, "I'm steadily getting better at what I do," your self-esteem will rise up, you'll feel better toward yourself, and your performance will leap forward too.

Here's another point related to this: if you're afraid of making mistakes and being seen as foolish in your intern work, you're not going to feel free to risk anything new – and that's a loss both for you and the company. As your self-esteem becomes stronger you'll be able to occasionally slip and do foolish things. But instead of cringing at what you did, you'll be able to learn from your mistakes and grow, perhaps even laugh at yourself.

And yeah, sometimes you'll need to make the same mistake a few times in order to learn the lesson – and that's perfectly alright. When you experience directly the downside of doing something foolish, you won't tend to do it again. There will also be others around you at work who now and then do something foolish – and you can certainly take note and learn from their mistakes. But there will always be challenging lessons that you must experience for yourself in order to get to the point where you change your behavior for the better.

> *Don't take yourself so seriously.*
> *No one else does.*
>
> **Regina Brett**

Playing The Right Game

It seems that our minds are built to learn certain patterns and behaviors during our childhood that we then repeat over and over as we move into adulthood. In the old days when life was very simple and change was relatively slow, following the patterns and behaviors we learned from our parents and local culture worked quite well for most of us – our inherited beliefs, attitudes, expectations and skills served us well throughout our lives.

But these days this has all changed. A life game that we inherited from our parents can in fact seem quite foolish when we're transported into an entirely different environment. When the rules and requirements change we must either learn to adapt to the new game – or fail. A lot of what happens in college is related to this issue of learning to play the right game for a new situation. And an internship can be doubly demanding at this core level.

It's certainly not easy to self-reflect to the extent that you can see the imprinted games you're playing in life, and then actively change them if they aren't appropriate to your new situation. But this is perhaps your deepest challenge to your success. I was playing the old games when I entered Princeton as an undergrad – I was following my parents' guidance to become a successful engineer. But step by step I realized that this game was not for me. I didn't want to play that game at all – and each year at Princeton reinforced that realization. I wanted very strongly to find a new game that was more to my liking and inclinations.

I should mention that we can continue playing the wrong game for years, even throughout our lifetime, and appear to be quite successful when viewed from our external financial situation. There are loads of people stuck in unfulfilling careers who play the old games magnificently. But they're personally quite unfulfilled because they're not fully utilizing their natural talents, they don't quite fit into the culture of their company, and deep inside they feel let down by their role in life, not raised up by it.

Here's the reality. You are always playing a game, even if you don't think you are. I'm not talking about gamification like the online trading companies are doing now. And I'm of course not talking about a board game or a sport. I'm talking about the game of life – the game that identifies who you are by the roles you're deeply immersed in.

You're presently playing the game of being a student – you're focused on academic rules and achievements within a limited playing field of opportunity. If you find this game extremely satisfying, perhaps you're headed for an academic profession. But if not, then ... what other game will you choose to identify with? And when you know the answer to that question, then what do you need to accomplish and learn in order to go out and actively begin being a player in that game?

I've personally chosen to play the game of entrepreneurship. It attracted me for years while I was playing the corporate financial game – and then when I reflected on this attraction adequately, I began to make moves in that general direction. I love coming up with new ideas and then providing a service or a product that makes a difference. I love the feeling of autonomy and personal responsibility, the roller-coaster ride that's part of any entrepreneurial venture. It's a very different game than being a corporate player. It has its ups and downs – and it's my chosen game.

When you go and do an internship, you're definitely playing a particular game. There are certain constraints and rules, obstacles and opportunities available in the game, and for a certain time period you're agreeing to play by those rules. You're experimenting to see if the game suits you enough to play it long-term. Meanwhile you also know that this is a game that will end. The intern game is special in that when the time frame of the game is over, you walk away and that's that.

Everybody who plays a game likes to win that game. We do play to win, even if it's a win-win. I encourage you to begin consciously defining for yourself what winning the intern game will look like for you. Keep reflecting on this question. Before, during and after your internship, you'll want to make sure to regularly pause and assess your inner feelings about how you are playing the game you're engaged in. And – you'll know you won the intern game if you have enjoyed the experience, have done good work, learned a lot, and have been acknowledged by your employer for your contributions.

In my company the game I play is win-win-win all the way for everyone. If each person in the game feels that they're winning, then we're playing the game correctly. For me, that's a far better game to play in business than any game where someone has to lose in order for me to win. The game I've chosen to play with my life is larger than my company. It includes my own family, my community, and my alma maters. For me, that's a game large enough to be worth playing.

Your intern assignment is to explore what games feel best to you. Look to see what game you're playing mostly on automatic right now in school. Then as you go and begin your internship, stay alert to how you feel about playing the game of that company. This is a great experiment! Be sure to look honestly to discover if the games you like to play are all about just you, or if you include the well-being of others in your game.

If your game is all about you, you'll probably come to realize at some point that it's a foolish game to play – because when people recognize the selfish game you're playing, they may not be interested in playing with you. That's deadening over time. However, you can choose to show up at your internship wanting to play a game that furthers your own evolution – and at the same time provides service, insight, compassion and other forms of support in the company. You'll be able to listen without judging, and be of help to your colleagues and the business as a whole. When you do this, your fellow workers will embrace your attitude and support your movement into your emerging career.

The only way to have a friend is to be one.

Ralph Waldo Emerson

Chapter Thirteen

FINAL THOUGHTS

~~~~~~~~~~~~~~~~~~

People of accomplishment rarely sit back
and let things happen to them.
They go out and happen to things.

Leonardo Da Vinci

On one level, you can look at the internship experience as an anxiety-filled rite of passage into our capitalist society – a dreaded requirement into the unknown world of employment. You might see interning as nothing more than a way to spend a college summer while you earn a little bit of much-needed money. When you think about interning this way, there isn't much at stake. Not so inspiring, is it?

My intention has been to share with you a way to elevate your view of internships to a bright new level where you can open up and experience the world of business as an exciting adventure. And it's all up to you. At this higher level, you present yourself authentically in the interview process, and even before beginning your internship you get busy preparing for your coming experience. You make the personal choice to get the most out of your internship. You also work on yourself to boost your self-esteem so that you approach interning confidently with minimum anxiety. You actively set yourself up for success.

Then while you're in your internship, you choose to learn everything you can about the company that's welcomed you into its internal operations. You explore the larger scope of the industry you're engaged with. And yes, even as an intern you choose to deliver quality work and to ask well-expressed questions that reflect your confidence, sincerity, compassion and sense of participation in the larger life of the company and industry.

Also you take your internship as a great chance to engage in a process of self-discovery. You regularly pause in your busy routine to examine your own thoughts and inner feelings. You learn ways to identify and then let go of attitudes and reactions that put you in an unproductive mood. You steadily develop your ability to work for a manager or with a team of co-workers in ways that build a solid foundation for your future.

The choice is always yours regarding how you take on your internship – as an opportunity for rapid learning, self-discovery, and joy … or an anxiety-laden required challenge you just want to survive and be done with. My hope is that the suggestions and insights in this book will assist you in letting go of the latter and fully embracing the former.

Always hold in mind that you are of value to your host company. You do have something of high value to contribute! You'll be in position to provide a fresh honest perspective to the company you're working for – and this is something that all businesses urgently need. Without honest insightful feedback it's impossible to improve in business. The same thing works the other way around of course – if you don't also stay open to receive honest feedback from your mentors, co-workers and clients, it's far too easy for you to go off in a fruitless direction. When open to receive feedback, you can evaluate, recalibrate and explore life in optimum directions. And remember that people tend to be more willing to hear your feedback when you are also open to receive constructive criticism, instruction and advice.

This last point is really important because in our society today both giving and receiving constructive criticism is becoming quite rare. Perhaps we've become overly defensive and also overly concerned of hurting others' feelings. Rather than improving our ability to both give and receive supportive feedback, we too often just shy away from such encounters. As a result, we can fail to grow in positive directions, both personally and professionally.

Through working with the self-reflection exercises in this book, you can begin expanding your self-awareness and evolving your ability to accept and understand your at-work habits. You can be more observant and kinder to those around you. You can listen to feedback without defending yourself, let go of mistakes and foibles that no one else will remember – and consciously course-correct for the better. You'll feel comfortable in your own skin even when another inevitable rough day happens.

Choosing To Be Of Value

As mentioned earlier, as an intern you come fresh into a situation that is new for you but often old and stagnant for the long-term employees and managers. This means you may be in an optimal position to observe, take note, reflect and comment on what happens and doesn't happen in your host company. From the beginning of your internship you can keep an eye on collecting and providing astute and constructive feedback – and your input (when offered in a kindly way) may end up positively impacting the future of the company.

Of course you'll want to regularly ask lots of questions in order to understand more fully what's happening around you, and more importantly why it's happening. Then, once you feel confident concerning what you've observed and analyzed, do take on the challenge of being a feedback provider – but only make this offering when people are ready to receive and process your opinions. Wait for the appropriate time or you'll run the risk of sounding arrogant or a know-it-all. When it's offered in the right constructive spirit, feedback can make a profound difference.

At the game level, regularly take an honest look – is this the game you want to play during your internship? Are you giving this game your all? Set your goal to be as open and honest as you can about everything going on around you and within you. Contribute as much positive energy, intelligence, compassion, hard work and insight as you can.

You can also include, in the scope and intent of your intern game, the challenge of making sure the next interns who come to your host company will have an even better experience than you did. Is there a structure you can put in place that will make it easier for next year's interns? Perhaps a guideline or informational booklet of who's who and what's what at the company would be a useful tool for future interns – use your imagination to make a difference. And of course make yourself available in the future to counsel new interns seeking information and advice.

You'll probably find a number of different games that you can envision and manifest in whatever role you get as an intern. Whatever new opportunities arise, choose to be an inspiring player who fully embraces feedback – and leave a wake of contribution in the process. If you get clear on what game you want to play, even before you arrive at your intern assignment you can embody your intern intentions so that you're a force that enlivens, inspires and at times leads those around you. Give up playing any game that keeps you from being an extraordinary authentic intern – continually on multiple levels, make the most of your time.

Playing the game of authenticity optimally starts before the interview process and continues through your engagement with your company. To win this game, at least once a week be sure to sit down with your journal and answer for yourself the following questions:

> *How am I doing?*

> *Am I taking advantage of all the opportunities that are coming my way – and if not, why not?*

Is my focus primarily absorbed with myself, or am I also focused on my team and the company as a whole?

Am I really playing the best game I know I can play here?

What might I do differently tomorrow and next week to expand my game to everyone's advantage?

Playing To Win-Win

Winning the authentic intern game – that's your challenge. For a brief period of your life, you're going to enter a company where everyone is already playing and mastering their own game at the company and in their lives. What a beautiful setting for you to play your authentic intern game!

I would like to end with two of my favorite quotes on games:

"Life's a game when it isn't.
And it's not a game, when it is."

"You are always winning
the game you are playing."

I've pondered these quotes for years. I invite you to do the same. Have a deeply fulfilling internship. And may all the games you choose to play in life – in your family, in your community, in your work – serve both you and those around you. Why? Because you truly deserve it. You are the future of business and all of life.

Enjoy your internship!

Let's Stay Connected

I welcome you to tune in to further programs, blogs, podcasts and other communications related to this empowerment theme and community. I also welcome your insights and suggestions, which you can send to me through the contact button found at:

www.AgileRainmakers.com

~~~~~~~~~~~~~~~~~~~~~~~~~~~~~~

Author Bio

~~~~~~~~~~~~~~~~~~~~~~~~~~~

Robert J. Khoury is the founder and CEO of Agile Rainmakers, a high-impact business development consulting and advisory firm based in Chicago's Gold Coast. His 20+year career in the financial industry has seen him in many roles: an equity derivatives trader, portfolio manager, corporate strategist, chief operating officer, recruiter, hedge fund executive, and private equity investor.

Rob earned a BSE in Electrical Engineering at Princeton University and his MBA from Duke University's Fuqua School of Business. He takes great pleasure in supporting college students and recent graduates in making career and life choices that support the fulfillment of their life's goals.

As a member of the Princeton Club of Chicago, for over a decade he has organized intern luncheons for Princeton students eager to find opportunities in Chicago. He has hired interns over the years and has a passion for ensuring their success.

Rob led personal and professional development seminars for Landmark Worldwide for several years; enjoys volunteering, philanthropy, and family vacations; and lives with his wife, Mary – a freshwater ecologist – and their two children in a downtown Chicago condo overlooking beautiful Lake Michigan. This book is the first in a series on internships.

~~~~~~~~~~~~~~~~~~~~~~~~~~~~~~~~